Lisa Maritz.

STRONG
WOMEN

SOFT
HEARTS

STRONG WOMEN

SOFT HEARTS

Paula Rinehart

W Publishing Group™
www.wpublishinggroup.com
A Division of Thomas Nelson, Inc.
www.ThomasNelson.com

Published by W Publishing Group, a Division of Thomas Nelson, Inc., P.O. Box 141000, Nashville,
Tennessee, 37214.

Many of the names used in this book have been changed to protect the privacy of those individuals.

Unless otherwise indicated, Scripture quotations are from the New American Standard Bible (NASB).
© The Lockman Foundation 1960, 1977.

Other Scripture references are from the following sources:

The Amplified Bible (AV), © The Lockman Foundation 1954, 1958, 1987.

The Holy Bible, New International Version (NIV). Copyright 1973, 1978, 1984 by International Bible
Society. Used by permission of Zondervan Publishing House. All rights reserved.

The Message (MSG), © 1993. Used by permission of NavPress Publishing Group.

The New King James Version (NKJV), © 1979, 1980, 1982, 1992 Thomas Nelson, Inc., Publishers.

Library of Congress Cataloging-in-Publication Data
Rinehart, Paula.
   Strong women, soft hearts / Puala Rinehart.
      p. cm.
   Includes bibliographical references.
   ISBN 0-8499-1674-7
      1. Middle aged women—Religious life. 2. Chritian women—Religious life. I. Title.
BV4579.5 .R54 2001
248.8'43—dc21

2001026138

Printed in the United States of America

01 02 03 04 05 PHX 7 6 5 4

*In memory of
Brent Curtis,
who first encouraged me
in this journey of the heart.*

CONTENTS

ACKNOWLEDGMENTS

For all the aloneness entailed in writing a book, there are so many people who influence both the author and the outcome. My special thanks for the contributions of the following people:

I am especially grateful to a small host of women who have shared their stories with me and in doing so, taught me more than they know. And to my colleagues, Dr. Peter van Dyck, Maria Lemons Wood, Bill Venable, and Jennifer Ennis.

To Jennifer Ennis, Virginia Huth, Eleanor Nagy, Connally Gillam, Dana Kozlarek, Ruth Brooks, and Sally Breedlove, my thanks for offering insight and helpful critique on various parts of this book.

To lifelong friends who serve with the Navigators, I am grateful for all they taught me of the privilege of knowing Christ and of having a life shaped by him.

To Maggie and Bob Wynne, for the generous use of their home in Montreat, North Carolina, a wonderful setting in which to write.

To Brennan Manning, for the gift of his spiritual direction and his encouragement to drink deeply at the well of God's love.

To Pam Monroe, for her willingness to share the wisdom she gained through such a dark and lonely time.

To Mark Sweeney and Laura Kendall at Word Publishing, for their confidence in this project.

To my mother, Polly Corn who has long modeled for me such a consistent example of strength.

And always, to my husband, Stacy, and our two children, Allison and Brady, my gratitude for encouraging and enduring a wife and mother who retreats for long hours to write.

THE JOURNEY
OF THE HEART

1

AWAKENING:
God Calls Our Hearts

In the end, it doesn't matter how well we have performed or what we have accomplished—a life without heart is not worth living. For out of this wellspring of our soul flow all true caring and all meaningful work, all real worship and all sacrifice.

BRENT CURTIS AND JOHN ELDREDGE

For all of a sudden when I saw those lights, I said to myself, Ivy, this is your life, this is your real life, and you are living it. Your life is not going to start later. This is it, it is now. It's funny how a person can be so busy that they forget this is it. This is my life.

LEE SMITH

T his book began to write itself a few years back, when I first washed up on the shores of midlife and wondered how I could feel so empty. People often complain of such things during that season of life—like someone drilled a hole through their souls. While everything looks the same on the outside, they feel hollow and restless, bored in ways that make no sense. For me, it was that very emptiness—the sense that something important was missing—that propelled me down this path. And for that I am incredibly grateful.

The emptiness pushed me in the direction of my heart. It moved me out of my head, where I kept trying to figure everything out, organizing it in piles neater than my walk-in closet. It forced me to leave all the busy rush of children's soccer games and places I must appear, and retreat for little bits of time to a still and quiet place where I could hear my soul again. The emptiness has a noise all its own, I discovered, a kind of piper's tune that begs you to pay attention. *Pay attention. This can take you somewhere good.*

It's strange the way we meander through life, thinking we are moving forward, only to discover that we have left our hearts behind.

More than a hundred years ago now, Frank Baum wrote a story for children we still read—the simple tale of a girl in Kansas caught up in a cyclone that carried her to a strange land called Oz. There Dorothy met up with a few other lost souls—a scarecrow who wanted someone to give him brains, a tin man in search of a heart, and a cowardly lion who lacked courage. Together they set off to see the wizard. Along the way they discovered what they felt they had so badly needed.

Frank Baum apparently never expected his story to be so popular. Adults have loved *The Wizard of Oz* nearly as much as children have through the years. And though Baum wrote other good books in his lifetime, he was forever pigeonholed as the man who created Dorothy and the cast of characters who inhabited the Emerald City. He never got too far from being the creator of Oz.

The reason I mention this story is that I think it tells a small but important truth about our lives. It gives a piece of all our stories. Dorothy and her friends captivate us, generation after generation, because we, too, are on a journey. Somehow we sense that becoming who we really are means that we also must discover our mind and heart and courage, or something crucial will be missing. The very struggles we would just as soon skip past become the ticket to gaining what we lack, as though God knew just the grist we needed to become what he had in mind.

Listening to the stories—the lives—of women, as a counselor and a writer, makes me very conscious of how similar our journeys are. Each

of us wants to become what I call a strong woman with a soft heart—
a woman in touch with God and alive to all the possibilities that walking with him can bring. It's just that sometimes we get mired in the very
clay he dug us out of, tangled in the weeds of our own wanderings.

Occasionally I meet a woman and listen to her story, and I find that I am the one who is changed from the encounter. A few years ago I spoke with a woman who had survived an operation no one thought she possibly could. Other than an occasional checkup, there

I find the temptation to shut down on the inside and settle for the crumbs under the table is one that every woman faces.

were no long-term effects on her health. In fact, the doctors said she
could do whatever she wanted to do. The problem was that five
years had passed and she still wasn't doing much of anything. She
had drawn a small circle around herself and she lived inside it—taking walks with an elderly mother, having lunch occasionally with
friends, cleaning her house. It was squeaky clean by this point. The
thought of actively engaging in life caused so much anxiety that she
stayed put, bound up with fear.

I asked the obvious question. What was she afraid of?

"I'm afraid I'm going to die," she said. Calamity had struck once
and she had survived. Calamity could strike again.

I kept thinking that she would see she had been graced with
another chance at life. That she would want to make the most of
the time God had given her. But weeks and weeks and weeks passed
and nothing budged. "You are going to die," I finally said one day
in a moment of quiet desperation. "The question it seems is, Are
you going to live?"

That question has returned to me a hundred times since I first
asked it. *Are you going to live?* And by that I mean, will you really
grab hold of life in whatever shape God has given it and live as
though you didn't go around twice? As simple as that sounds, I find

the temptation to shut down on the inside and settle for the crumbs under the table is one that every woman faces. It's a temptation I face. We can so easily sleepwalk through our days—out of touch, disconnected, half-alive. We can die before our time, really. On the inside, we can die long before there are any visible signs.

The underlying premise of this book is that we must have our hearts intact in order to make the journey of life well. We must have access to the inside stuff—the longings and desires and dreams and vulnerabilities that make us who we are. God placed those in us. He means for us to live from the heart. It's the place where we first hear his voice and respond. It's the key to so much—to trust and the willingness to forgive; to laughter, wisdom, and sacrifice; to being able to love others in a real way.

Life is not a journey you want to make on autopilot.

FOLLOWING THE TRAIL

Suppose someone pulled you aside and said, "Tell me about the moments in your life when you felt really alive." What would you say?

- Would you recount for them the experience of holding your first child in your arms?
- Would you describe, perhaps, what it feels like to sit for an hour and look out over a mountain ridge at the glory of fall colors?
- How about the memory of a laugh-till-you-cry story with a good friend?
- Or the moment when the same old argument you've had for years with your husband suddenly broke through to a new level of understanding?
- Would you talk about a time when you could sense the presence of God in some very real way?

Simple moments like these, which we string together like pearls on a necklace, are more important than we realize. They are sure clues to the capacity of our hearts to engage in life in an open and unguarded way. But if we have been burned at some point, seared by the pain of life, we tend to close off the chambers of our souls until our hearts are frozen in place, hard and impenetrable. The effort to shield ourselves from pain also blocks our awareness of the good stuff. And then, unfortunately, we could be standing knee-deep in a river of water and feel that we are dying of thirst. Our hearts are unable to receive.

Sometimes I find that a woman's clearest memories of feeling really alive come from childhood. One friend recounted for me how, when she was six years old, she would fill her mother's pickle jar full of water and sit for hours in the Oklahoma sun, shaping red clay into her first pottery. It was something close to bliss, she said. All the wonder and innocence of childhood was still in place. She didn't have to have life packaged with a bow. She could trust that good would come to her in the right time. She was simply there on the hillside, creating something she thought was beautiful.

All of us have memories like this, tucked away in the attic of our minds. Times when we led the parade. When our dreams were still intact. When we could still be amazed by a butterfly's wings. And we think, somehow, that growing up means letting that go. When we start to get beaten up by life a bit, those original hopes and long-ings are often knocked from our arms. So we pick them up and pack them away, out of sight, where it doesn't hurt too much to remember. And we go on.

It's terribly important, though, that we don't just go on. Please don't just go on. Instead, reclaim your heart, then go back and ask God for the *essence* of your original hopes and dreams, the ones he means for you to carry into the future. They are necessary to make the journey well.

Of course, childhood is not the only place where we are free to listen to our hearts. My heart was engaged in a way close to the way it was in childhood when I was first introduced to Christ. That's a good way to describe the experience because it is like meeting someone for the first time. Then you discover that he has always known you, better even than you know yourself. Christ touched the tender, hopeful, childlike place in my heart. Or to put it another way, he blew the lock off the door and I sensed a powerful freedom in him I had not known before.

The distance grows between our heads and our hearts and we lose our felt connection with the presence of God.

It is a bit of a mystery how we lose the early glow we have when the wonder of the gospel first captures us. How we slowly drift from the domain of the heart to a focus on efficiency and performance—as though this whole thing was mostly about doing and duty. The passion is replaced with just showing up. And before long, we have struck a kind of macabre contract with God, and we hope that if we just keep the rules, the road will rise to meet us. And we will be spared the pain. The distance grows between our heads and our hearts and we lose our felt connection with the presence of God.

If I am honest, I admit that I let that distance build through the years. My heart was a mysterious bundle of needs and fears and longings I could not name. It seemed to be dangerous territory I should avoid. I remembered well Jeremiah's warning that the heart was deceitful and sick[1]—only later did I realize that he was speaking of the unredeemed heart and how desperate and crazy the search for life becomes when it's not a search for life in God. I used words like Jeremiah's as an excuse to steer clear of much that looked at the inner life. But the truth is, I was scared. I simply closed the door on it all. Exploring how I felt or what I longed for was a venture into the great unknown. It took the emptiness to get my attention. In the emptiness I could hear God knocking—and what he was knocking on, I slowly realized, was the door to my heart.

As I talk with women, it is apparent that my experience is not unique. We often avoid, as long as we can, any serious grappling with the life of the heart. We waltz past our losses, bury our feelings, and try to pretend. Two barriers loom large. We fear our hearts as dangerous havens of something that could undo us. Or we perceive the domain of the heart as one of weakness, the source of an emotional softness that would allow us to be taken advantage of by others. Actually, it is neither.

THE VULNERABILITY OF WOMEN

At the center of being a woman lies a paradox that can help us understand why we often find living from the heart a precarious venture.

On one hand, we possess a rather wonderful capacity for relationship. Our language is that of the heart—experiencing life deeply, feeling connected to those we love, enjoying the ambiance. This capacity enriches our lives immeasurably. That's the good news.

The bad news is that this very capacity also makes us more vulnerable to loss. You can't make a relationship happen like you would make up your mind to start a business or achieve some tangible goal. Relationships, and really most matters of the heart, are inherently more unmanageable. Relationships defy our attempts at control. The people we love don't always love us back. Friends move away. Lovers change. And the truth is that if we live long enough, we face the potential loss of everyone who matters to us.

So the very capacity that provides our ticket to the richest moments of life—to the most meaningful connection with God and with those we love—also riddles our lives with risk. Our greater capacity for relationship opens up a larger possibility for experiencing pain. The secret of our hearts is that we can be touched. We can be moved deeply. Simply put, *we can be gotten to.*

On a deep level, then, we face a choice about what we will do with that pain. Many a woman opts for letting go of her passion for life and relationship so that she has less to risk. She builds walls instead of bridges. She lets her heart shrink on the inside and the shell grows tough. The alternative, of course, is to let the pain and loss associated with the world of relationships become a tool in the hand of God, to actually shape a new sort of strength and vitality so that we have even more to give.

Vulnerability is key if we are to understand how we so easily move through life, leaving our hearts behind. It happens in ways you might recognize.

We Live Other People's Stories, Not Our Own

When I first met Anna, I wondered at how much she had going for her—and how depressed she was. In her late twenties, with an enviable job and many friends, Anna had been stopped in her tracks by a general malaise that would not lift. She found herself, for the first time, unmotivated and at loose ends with life.

Her story tumbled out easily. The steps of Anna's life had been carefully scripted, and in many ways it was a good plan. She would attend certain schools, date a certain kind of guy, and eventually become an interior designer like her mother. Anna had followed the yellow brick road well. She and her mother now owned a small, thriving company. Family pressure, though, had been just strong enough to keep Anna from asking the necessary open-ended questions about her life. So I asked one for her, the simplest one. What did she want to do with her life?

"I haven't really let myself ask that question," she admitted. And then in a quieter voice she added, "Sometimes I wonder if I have been living my mother's life—not mine."

This is such a common refrain for women. We tend to pick up on others' expectations—not just our mothers'—and shape ourselves to fit a preordained mold. We aim to please. And in the process, it takes us longer to uncover our own opinions or make choices for which we take responsibility. We get the story of our lives lost in someone else's.

The way this happens is a bit like an old story told about a mother and daughter discussing the daughter's upcoming wedding plans. Her mother wanted classical music, and she thought pink roses made the loveliest flowers for such

That is what each of us needs to be able to say— I am doing what I was born for.

an occasion. And she knew just the photographer. The cake should have fresh flowers, and on and on. "Wait a minute," the daughter finally said. "This is my wedding. You already had your wedding."

Her mother thought for a minute and then replied, "No . . . actually I had *my* mother's wedding."

It's kind of a funny story, until you realize that we can live our whole lives like this. When we do, we miss the necessary step of sitting before the Lord and listening with our hearts for some sense of direction meant personally for us. I will never forget the response of a woman who, after a history of painful miscarriages, volunteered a day a week to help other women who had experienced infertility or the loss of children. She now had two small children of her own, so I asked how she managed to give her time in this busy season of life.

She looked at me as if I were clueless. "You don't understand," she replied. "When I help women through this painful experience I feel like I am doing something I was born for."

That is what each of us needs to be able to say—*I am doing what I was born for.* And that requires a trip inside, into the world of the heart, where we let ourselves ask questions that don't have to be quickly answered and we can weigh out possibilities with wisdom. As the poet Herb Gardner wrote,

> You have to own your days, every one of them,
> Or else the years go by and none of them belong to you.[2]

We Create a Miniature Version of the Story We're Meant to Live

There is a story from the years following the thawing of the Soviet Union that mirrors well how we come to live lives smaller than the ones we long for.

A group of Lithuanian teachers was offered the opportunity to come to this country to relax at a retreat center for a few weeks, courtesy of a few generous Texans. These teachers had never been out of their country—many had not been more than thirty miles from the gray, high-rise government apartments they knew as home.

As you can imagine, this was a dream come true for these women. They boarded a plane that carried them halfway around the world to a place awash with color and sun, fresh fruits and vegetables, opportunities at every hand. There were no restrictions here. They could explore to their hearts' content. They had been given, essentially, the keys to the city. As the week progressed, though, a strange situation unfolded. No one knew quite what to make of it. Two of these women never left their rooms. They remained there most of the week, too afraid to venture out.

Fear can have this kind of paralyzing effect on anyone. We allow fear to reduce the world to a couple of small rooms, where things are known and familiar and we feel in control. In this miniature version of our lives, we accept the status quo in our closest relationships and don't ask for too much. Or we settle for jobs that won't stretch us. We go through the motions in our spiritual lives, but our hearts are not in it. Like these two Lithuanian teachers, we are surrounded by wonderful opportunities, yet we miss what's really there.

When I limit myself to the small rooms of life, I find myself mired in the small stuff of life. Small conversations about someone else's goings and doings with a little piece of gossip thrown in for size. Small shopping trips to collect more small stuff to be cleaned and dusted. When I am honest, though, I know that's not what my heart wants. I remember how clearly Jesus said there is no real life in all that stuff.[3] But it is easy to get taken in by the mirage.

Living the smaller version of what we're meant to live is, essentially, a response to pain. Sometimes the painful happenings of our lives are our own doing. I think of a young wife who avoided sexual intimacy because it triggered memories of the guilt and loss she felt after an abortion chosen in a desperate moment during her freshman year in college. She almost invented arguments with her husband in order to keep the distance between them—even though she hated what was happening to her marriage. But her life stayed stuck in this tight place until her heart could be softened by the experience of forgiveness.

Some of our wounds, though, are inflicted by others. A husband walks off after twenty-five years of marriage and you are left to pick up the pieces. Or a drunk driver leaves you with months of physical therapy and a stack of bills. Or the sexual abuse suffered at the age of twelve becomes the reason you stay clear of men. It is easy to build small lives around the pain we encounter, to get lost in one thread of the plot of the story and miss the big theme. We can, unfortunately, build a monument to our woundedness. We can shape an identity around the things we've suffered. But somewhere in this, our hearts become frozen in place and the real life God has given becomes hidden, even to us.

The shrinking of our lives is like living in a beautiful old home, where we are meant to have access to every room and fresh breezes blowing throughout—only our response to the pain of life is to let guilt and fear and shame take up residence there, until we quietly shut the door to room after room of our souls. There's nowhere left to live, except perhaps the front parlor where we receive guests who are never invited in much farther, and with whom we exchange only polite pleasantries. All the while, we wonder how on earth we have come to be so lonely.[4]

That is the tragedy of becoming a stranger to your own heart.

THE HEART OF GOD

All of this begs an essential question: How does the awakening of our hearts change the way we experience a walk with God? And even more important, does he care? Does this matter to him?

I remember standing in St. Isaac's Cathedral in St. Petersburg once and feeling awash with the majesty of God. Beautiful paintings depicting classic Bible stories filled the walls—a visual feast to the illiterate eyes of Russian peasants from another century. Incense and music enveloped me. I have never been more tangibly aware of the splendor of a high and holy God. Worship is really the only rational response we can have to beauty of this magnitude. Perhaps those who built St. Isaac's knew better than most of us what David meant when he said that he sought one thing only— that he might behold the beauty of the Lord.[5]

But there is another aspect of that beauty that awes. That this high and holy God, who owes us nothing, would come in search of us—now that is worth stopping in your tracks to absorb. He pursues us past all our talent and hard work into the secret places of our hearts where sin and inadequacy and brokenness hide, and he rejoices to claim us there as his own. Even there, where we least expect to find him. God circles our lives, I think, like a king circles

the walls of a castle, looking for points of entrance. There is someone on the other side he desires. The English poet George Herbert
must have felt the wonder of this when he wrote:

> My God, what is a heart
> that thou shouldst it so eye, and woo,
> Pouring upon it all thy art,
> As if thou hadst nothing else to do?[6]

This high and Holy God seeks the intimacy of the human heart.

While we meet the face of God in Jesus, it is in the Old
Testament that we most hear his heart. Only the Hebrew experience is strong enough to bear the weight of love this faithful, this
relentless. In the words that
Handel chose to begin his
Messiah, God tells a messenger
to climb the highest mountain
and literally shout: Here is your
God! It is as though God himself
cries, "Here I am! Can't you see
me? Can't you hear my heart?"

The fact that God can be moved . . . tells us more than anything else how much our hearts matter to him.

God comes to us with his passionate heart on display—grieved
that we have abandoned our love affair with him. He is the Father
we ran away from, the Great King before whom we are loath to
bow. He goes to such lengths to find us. Yet we recognize him in
one way only—when he is hung on an old Roman cross beneath
a darkened sky at midday.

"I marvel at a God who puts himself at our mercy, as it were,
allowing himself to be quenched and grieved, and even forgotten,"
wrote Philip Yancey.[7] Indeed, it is amazing that the Holy One of
Israel would let himself be affected by our affections. The fact that
God can be moved—that he would allow our indifference to bring

him grief and anger, our trust to bring him joy—tells us more than anything else how much our hearts matter to him. "Trust is our gift back to God, and he finds it so enchanting that Jesus died for love of it."[8] It is the longing of God's heart for ours that draws us home.

Knowing God, then, has to be about more than adhering to a set of principles or behaviors—even though, goodness knows, it is tempting to reduce it all to that. But anyone can learn the tenets of belief in God or follow a set of rules. What melts our wills is a hope much larger, one that seems too good to be true. It is the hope that the One who spoke the worlds into being would want us.

> What he is after is us—our laughter, our tears, our dreams, our fears, our heart of hearts. Remember his lament in Isaiah, that though his people were performing all their duties, "their hearts are far from me." How few of us truly believe this. We've never been wanted for our heart, our truest self, not really, not for long. The thought that God wants our heart seems too good to be true.[9]

That God would set his affection on us—that he would want our hearts—is what gives us courage on this journey, which leads somewhere far better than Kansas or the Emerald City.

For many years now, the focus of my husband's life has been world missions. The conversations around our dinner table tend to span the globe. We talk about what God is doing in the big picture of it all. God's heart for the world he created is so clear: For God so loved the *world* that he gave his Son.

By some touch of irony, though, I also sit and listen to the stories of individuals—often in pain, and usually at a loss as to which way to turn. There I see a different aspect of God and his tender, doggedly persistent pursuit of the individual heart. His Spirit chases us down and shines light into every nook and cranny of our souls, as though they mattered—as though we mattered, and infinitely so.

Wonderful Counselor is one of his names. It awes me equally that God could love the whole world, and yet care passionately about the whole heart of one single individual. I never cease to be amazed.

So our hearts are of central importance to God. Like small violins beneath the chin of a great master, we are tuned so that we are able to hear his heart. From our hearts we offer him the worship he is so rightly due. "Listen carefully to Me, and eat what is good. . . . Listen, that you may live."[10] It is with our hearts that we listen to him.

What God asks of us is both simpler and more profound than adherence to a system of beliefs or following a set of rules. He asks us to walk with him through the blood and guts of our real experience in an honest pilgrimage where we let him show us what real strength, and real love, are all about.

Listen with Your Heart

1. Take a few moments and a blank sheet of paper and write about one memory of when you felt most alive.

2. What most tempts you to make the journey of your life on autopilot?

3. The Old Testament story of Joseph is a wonderful example of someone who was able to hold on to the original dream God gave him, in spite of all he encountered—being sold into slavery, prison, the loss of home. In Genesis 45:8–10, read his words to his brothers after they discovered him in Egypt. What evidence do you see here that Joseph continued to trust the promises God had originally given him?

4. On the last day of the Feast of Booths, Jesus stood before his listeners, and the Bible says he "cried out" an invitation to come to him. Read John 7:37–38. How do you hear his promise? What does that mean to you?

5. What do you think Herb Gardner meant when he said that you have to "own your days," or else the years go by and they don't belong to you?

6. Consider God's complaint about the heart of his people as expressed in Isaiah 29:13. How would you describe the gap between the external part of their lives and what was happening inside? In what way does this motivate you?

7. When are you most aware of God's heart for you?

8. What has drawn you personally to a focus on the journey of the heart? What is this need about in your own life?

2

DESIRE:
The Language of the Heart

For I have known them all already, known them all—
Have known the evenings, mornings, afternoons,
I have measured out my life with coffee spoons.

T. S. ELIOT

Our Lord finds our desires not too strong, but too weak. We are half-
hearted creatures, fooling about with drink and sex and ambition when
infinite joy is offered us, like an ignorant child who wants to go on mak-
ing mud pies in a slum because he cannot imagine what is meant by the
offer of a holiday at sea. We are far too easily pleased.

C. S. LEWIS

Lord, all my desire is before Thee; and my sighing is not hidden from Thee.

PSALM 38:9

I really enjoy helping women sort through one of the great questions of their lives: *Do I love this man and should I marry him?* If I could become one of those old Jewish matchmakers like the little nosy lady you see in *Fiddler on the Roof*, I might apply for the job. Some women know when they've found the guy they want to

19

marry. And others sweat bullets trying to decide. One woman, Marie, helped me see how crucial the role of desire is in this decision, as in all of life. And how dangerous it is to fail to listen to your heart.

Marie had always fallen for guys who were really sharp—men who were going places and wanted to take her along. The kind of guy you brought into a group of friends and other women pulled you aside and asked if he had a brother. The trouble was that none of these relationships had ended very well. One guy had just stopped calling with no explanation. Another cheated on her. And the last especially charming one had inspired a period of sharp weight loss she didn't need by insisting that she looked a bit pudgy.

If the previous men in her life had been strawberry trifle, the guy Marie had been seeing for the past few months was good old granola. What he lacked in polish and sophistication, he made up for in reliability. He was solid, stable—a sharp contrast to Marie's father, who so often made promises he did not keep. But Marie's friends wondered at the match. "He's not like any of the other guys you've been interested in," they said. Marie thought that might be a stroke in his favor!

I asked her if she knew what she really wanted in a man. What was important to her? What did a good man even look like? I encouraged her not to avoid the qualities in a guy that had been hurtful in the past, as though she had developed some strange allergy to sharp, attractive men. She could be running away from something all her life on that basis.

She shouldn't make any big decision in her life out of fear, I told her. In so much of life, wisdom is fundamentally about making a choice based on desire.

Desire is a strange animal. It lies at the center of things—and yet, at times, it seems to be the villain that gets us into a peck of trouble. We come into the world crying our heads off—wanting, needing, desiring. Everything we do from then on is about needing or wanting something. We are painfully incomplete. What we do with that shapes the story of our lives. Desire—longing—can lead us home to God. It can bring us into the arms of those we love. And sometimes, it can send us right over the edge of the proverbial cliff.

The language of the heart is the language of desire. It's everywhere you turn. For instance, when you tour a friend's new house, you will be happy for her—and you may also feel a pang of envy. Sometimes a longing shows up first in that strange green form. If your husband takes you on a special trip, you know the last day will be a bear—you want to stay in this idyllic place forever. If your teenager is determined to learn everything the hard way, you may long for the day when he used to curl up in your lap.

All of this is to say that the heart is a bundle of longings and desire. It's as though we still have a memory of the Garden of Eden, and we are homesick for something we just can't quite get our hands around here. These longings are the holes in our soul. They tell us something important—that we need God. We need God and we are not gods ourselves. And that's a big difference. These longings are not meant to go away this side of heaven. "We are like Swiss cheese, and the holes in us are actually supposed to be there. The holes are the things that make us who we are. The holes are the places God has reserved in us for Himself! The longings identify our real hunger. A hunger that drives us to Him to be satisfied."[1]

We are painfully incomplete. What we do with that shapes the story of our lives.

C. S. Lewis once remarked that God is so masculine, we are all feminine in comparison to him. What he meant is that we don't initiate anything. We are responders to light and love that is not our own. We are all moons. The majestic power of God that made the heavens and formed the earth, also reaches into the core of our being and shapes our very spirit. As Zechariah said,

Thus declares the LORD who stretches out the heavens, lays the foundation of the earth, and forms the spirit of man within him.[2]

God made our spirit to respond to him—to hunger and desire beyond ourselves that which is wholly other, Holy Other. He made us incomplete—with gaps, holes, yearnings, desires that woo us to our real home. We make a big mistake if we toss our longings away lightly.

In his book *The Journey of Desire,* John Eldredge asks a rather shocking question. I had to think about it for a while. When, Eldredge says, do you ever see Jesus accusing someone of wanting too much?[3] When does Jesus rebuke someone for desiring? If anything, you see just the opposite. Jesus actually fanned the flames of desire. To the woman with five husbands who thought she was simply in search of a jar of water, Jesus skipped past the superficial and poked and prodded her on the level of desire. He said she should ask for the real thing—living water. She didn't have to settle for the kind of water, the love of men, that would always evaporate and leave her more thirsty. Unless Christ exposed her desire, she would never find him.

When the blind man stopped Jesus on the road to Jericho, Jesus answered his simple request for mercy with a startling question of his own. "What do you want Me to do for you?" he asked. As though Jesus didn't know! Christ waited for him to put his desire into plain words: "I want to regain my sight."[4]

Christ took him back to his desire—or rather, he brought the desire of his heart into plain view, front and center.

Desire is your heart on a plate. We are nowhere in this thing of following Christ—and we will never know our own hearts—if we manage to deaden ourselves to desire. As Eldredge says,

> This may come as a surprise to you: Christianity is not an invitation to become a moral person. It is not a program for getting us into line or for reforming society. . . . At its core, Christianity begins with an invitation to desire.

Christianity has nothing to say to the person who is completely happy with the way things are. Its message is for those who hunger and thirst—for those who desire life as it was meant to be.[5]

God is a passionate being, and the Bible is the canvas of his passion. When he created the world, the morning stars sang for joy, a symphony of praise. God's anger breaks the rocks into pieces; his love is a consuming fire. It is the joy of reigning with the Father that enabled Jesus to face the cross. We cannot hope to grow more like Christ without discovering the depths of passion and longing. *Christianity begins with an invitation to desire.* Exploring the desire of our hearts is not a waste of time. It is precisely the place where God is stirring.

It is the golden cord of our connection to God—and to each other.

SEEING DESIRE AS THE ENEMY

I confess that I would not always have seen this to be true. Like many people, I saw desire as the enemy. In my mind, a longing was something you just got over. It is a common mistake, I find, to hear Christ's words to "deny yourself" and let go of the wrong things, all the while keeping what we actually need to surrender.

I engaged not in the practice of self-denial that Jesus taught, but in something more akin to the darker process of self-annihilation. I grew suspect of my creativity and my artsy bent, so I buried it. I had always been someone who liked nothing so much as a new idea. I would rather think than eat. But doing, not thinking, seemed to be the valuable thing in Christian circles, and so I let that part of my soul go to sleep. I was wired like an English major in a fraternity of spiritual engineers, and without consciously admitting it, whatever there was about me that didn't fit the norm, I labeled as wrong.

Gratefully, I was awakened by a sense of boredom that seemed out of place in following Jesus and by a restlessness I could not cure. Something was wrong. Boredom and Jesus—that was like oil and water. It struck me that, clearly, I had missed a few important turns on this journey.

As I retraced my own steps, the instructions to Wormwood in C. S. Lewis's *Screwtape Letters* were like light in the fog. Screwtape reminds the junior devil:

> Remember, always, that He really likes the little vermin, and sets an absurd value on the distinctness of every one of them. When He talks of their losing their selves, He means only abandoning the clamor of self-will; once they have done that, He really gives them back all their personality, and boasts that when they are wholly His they will be more themselves than ever.[6]

When we are wholly his we will be more ourselves than ever. What an incredible thought! The more completely we belong to Christ, the more of our real selves we become. Reclaiming my heart in the sense of owning my longings has been like entering a pantry and finally getting the labels on the right jars. To a greater extent, I have God's permission to live out the truth of who I am—to believe that my desires are not an accident, a mistake, or a nuisance. It is the definition of joy to be able to offer back to God the essence of what he's placed in you, be that creativity or a love of ideas or a compassionate heart or the gift of hospitality.

I am convinced that owning our longings and trusting God with those is crucial in bringing the color and music back into our lives.

Our human tendency in the whole idea of self-denial is to let go of the wrong stuff—repent of the wrong things. Longings, desires, passions, personality—these things are innate, God-given, his idea. They are not the primary stuff of repentance. The real villain is more willful. *I will make it happen—my idea, my way, my timing.*

Self-will always dispenses with trust. And when we won't trust God, we take matters into our own hands.

It's as though God has given each of us a song to sing, and he is the choir director. He motions when it's time to sound our notes and when to keep silent. He knows exactly how the song needs to be sung. We don't want to make the mistake of repenting of the song itself. He lays desires and longings on our hearts. The song, then, is what we sing to his glory.

Many women would identify with the struggle of owning their desires. And while trying to erase or stamp out desire inevitably leads to some kind of misery, there are subtle rewards that, unfortunately, make the practice strangely attractive—as we will see.

WHAT WE DO WITH DESIRE

Most of us suffer considerable ambivalence about our desires and longings. On one hand, how exactly will we get along without them? Who can carve out much of a life in the absence of passion and desire?

And yet, it's scary to turn around and face them. Suppose you feel the urge to run off with the postman? Or you share your dream with a friend and she says the equivalent of, "Honey, get a grip." You may risk your heart to realize something you have always wanted . . . and watch it slip through your fingers. Longings can lead to disappointment, and that is not much fun. No wonder we avoid dealing with desire.

There are two directions we tend to turn with desire, and both of them lead us away from our own hearts.

Deadening Desire

The most common way to handle desire is to find a way to deaden it, to pretend it doesn't exist. We reduce desire to a level we can manage and control.

Alice had no real complaint about her life, even though she felt depressed most of the time. Her days went by in a blur. She hadn't felt joy for so long she could hardly remember the emotion. But she functioned well—so well that hardly anyone in the school where she taught, or her husband and friends, would guess how down she felt. She organized children's church as she had for years. Like the Energizer Bunny, she kept going . . . and going . . .

There was one small glitch, though—an estrangement from her oldest son. He had fallen in love with a girl of whom Alice and her husband deeply disapproved. Their disapproval was strong enough to force a watershed choice: Either the son would give up the relationship or he would give up his family. He chose the girl. And a few months later, he moved in with her. For four years, Alice had barely laid eyes on him. But she went on about her business and accepted this awful state of affairs as simply the way things were.

But our hearts, if we can still hear them, will always lead us in the direction of weathering the pain and salvaging relationships.

"Don't you miss your son?" I asked her. "How are you living with him right in the same town, and yet birthdays and holidays go by and he is not in the picture? Don't you want to work this out?"

Alice looked at me strangely. She thought for a moment. "When it all first happened, I felt terrible. But I couldn't change his mind. And so I guess I just let it go. I tell myself I have to just move on."

It's no wonder that Alice was depressed. It takes a phenomenal amount of energy to deaden a mother's desire to see her son. Children can make incredibly disappointing choices. And riding out the effects of those choices with them turns the darkest head of hair gray. But our hearts, if we can still hear them, will always lead us in the direction of weathering the pain and salvaging relationships. Our desires will help us do the hard work of stating our concerns truthfully, while still holding tight to the ties that bind us together as family.

This thing of deadening desire looks so foolish, and so difficult, you have to wonder why we do it. Yet all of us move in this direction at times.

Disowning desire saves us from having to wade through some really difficult places in our lives. When we deaden desire,

- We don't have to face the disappointment of a lost dream;
- We save ourselves from doing the slow and tedious work of repairing a broken relationship;
- We don't have to sweat through trusting God with the things we don't understand; and
- We can avoid, a little longer, our fear of what others will think.

If we can convince ourselves that we don't want, we won't hurt. For a while, at least. We can take the whole stinking mess, shove it in a closet, and lock the door. And then we convince ourselves that we no longer care. Of course, that defies all the laws of the heart. Those desires pound on the closet door and demand attention. They make their appearance in aberrant forms: depression, anxiety, addictions. They do *not* go away. That would require nothing short of a heart transplant.

I am often reminded of the Proverb, "There is a way that *seems* right to a man, but its end is the way of death."[7] And when we deaden ourselves to desire, a lot that's good and right and true in us dies in the process.

The insidious part about deadening desire is that in some circles it brings applause. We call a passionless person by other names. We say she is a stable, responsible soul. Those who have given up all claim to desire are sometimes called godly—so sanctified they do not want a thing. Some feel the only way they can serve God is to keep all their desires at the lowest level possible. But God does not deaden desire—rather, he awakens desire and transforms it. And that's hugely different. "Killing desire may look like sanctification, but it's really godlessness. Literally, our way of handling life without God."[8]

Misplaced Passion

The other way we deal with desire is much more familiar. We become addicted—to a relationship, a substance, a state of being.

Addiction is a strong word, one usually connected with smoking or drugs or too much alcohol. But suppose we talk about it in less drastic terms—say, being overly attached. Attachment comes from the French word *attaché,* which means "nailed to." In addiction or attachment, our desires are nailed to a specific object. I think of it as having my heart captured. And in that sense, I know that I am no stranger to addiction.

Take antiques, for instance. I have always loved a good antique. At times, I can say that I am too attached—nailed to—hunting for them. That may not sound like much of an addiction to you, but trust me, where I live there is an antique under every rock and each one has its pull. I find even the smell of an antique shop is soothing. Antiques offer a hidden bait, an invisible trail back into history. A piece that is turn-of-the-century can be traded or resold for one made in the mid-1800s. On and on the process goes until you actually own the gold standard: a period antique. Not that I do, but the holy grail is always there. I can, if I let myself, pour my life into hunting for antiques.

My point, really, is that our hearts can be captured by almost anything. When a person is attached to a substance like drugs or alcohol, the addiction is tangible and easy to see. But most addictions are like my bout with antiques—they seem to be part of the landscape.

To keep my sanity and my wallet intact, I may have to walk out of an actual antique shop, but I must move deeper into the question of desire. Most addictions are that way. They cannot be broken by sheer will power. Recovery is always about the actual reclaiming of desire.

When I become obsessed with antiques, I can only break through the mirage by asking myself what I really want. *What am I really after here?* If I continue to peel back the layers of desire, I discover that my fascination with antiques is the front edge of a longing for home. For a place outside the material world that will always be there; where everything is secure and I know I am loved. Once I own my true desire, the illusion begins to evaporate. An antique can never deliver something that good.

A measure of freedom slowly enters the picture. The faint whispers of Christ grow more distinct. I can actually hear them now, inviting me to find my home in him. I really can come *home*. I suppose that if I live to be eighty, I will still enjoy a good antique shop—though by that time, I will be an antique. The hope of keeping my heart intact and my shopping within bounds will come from seeing through my desire until I discover the real thing—and move toward him. It will be about embracing desire, not disowning it.

Addictions get their fuel from leeching off of our true desires. No one wants a hangover, really. Or an empty checking account. Or feeling your every move is dictated by your attraction to another person. We are always after something more. As Gerald May explains,

> Addiction exists wherever persons are internally compelled to give energy to things that are not their true desires. . . . Psychologically, addiction *uses up* desire. It is like a psychic malignancy, sucking our life energy into specific obsessions, leaving less and less energy available for

other people and other pursuits. Spiritually, addiction is a deep-seated form of idolatry. The objects of our addictions become our false gods. These are what we worship, what we attend to, where we give our time and energy, *instead of love*. Addiction, then, displaces and supplants God's love as the source and object of our deepest true desire.[9]

Addictions usually get their start at some earlier point of significant pain. I once knew a woman who had struggled for years with food. Her moods were dictated by what she'd eaten—or not eaten. The self-hatred that ensued when she had one Oreo too many was the very thing that made her go back for the whole pack. But it is no surprise that her emotional life centered around food. When she was eleven, her father left home for the last time. She discovered his departing note propped against the milk carton in the refrigerator. She, then, had to deliver the bad news to her mother. Is it any wonder that the object of dark fascination was food?

Ironically, when this woman began to peel back the layers of desire she discovered that what she really wanted was not food, but real and meaningful time with her husband. She longed for someone to share her life with. The refrain in her mind, though, had always been that her husband was too busy and that she expected too much.

She slowly began to move in the direction of her real desire. "What can we do together?" she would ask. They began to talk as they hadn't talked in years. And she discovered that a few cookies were enough. They were not, after all, the thing she had actually wanted, but only the consolation prize.

RECLAIMING DESIRE

So . . . what do you want?

It's a scary question, isn't it? But it's also an oddly hopeful one. To think that God himself would invite you to step into the territory of your desire—that it's not too much for him to handle, too dangerous for you to explore, or too petty to concern him—is incredible. Desire and longing are the raw stuff he shapes in the secret chambers of your soul. They are our ticket to a passionate, meaningful life—and to knowing God.

In this journey of desire, there is actual movement, as though you are traveling somewhere, but the destination is not on any map. The best way I know to describe it is that you move out of the stands and onto the playing field. In the

What would you begin to do if you thought you could?

stands, you are just a spectator, watching your own life, a passive onlooker to a game where other people call the plays. You are what someone else says you are. It's the turtle story, where a hard shell protects all the live stuff inside. But you can only stay in the stands so long without the soul-numbing sense that you are missing your own life.[10] The only one God gave you.

To move from being a spectator is to step out on the field and risk banging up your knees a bit. To experience the muddy, sweaty exhilaration of actually playing the game. What would you begin to do if you thought you could? Would you want to live in a foreign country? Or begin a ministry no one else had attempted? Or write a book? Or plant a perennial garden? Or ask your mother-in-law if there wasn't some way to mend the deafening silence between you?

Where would desire take you if you didn't douse the flame of possibility before someone else attempted to blow it out? If you didn't rain on your own parade?

Desire is the tug of your heart to get in the game. I wish I could tell you that God would fulfill all your desires, but then we would be talking not about God, but about a genie in a bottle. God knows what you need, really. He says, simply,

> Delight yourself in the LORD;
> And He will give you the desires of your heart.[11]

At first glance that sounds as though God has promised to fulfill all your dreams. But a careful reading brings us closer to reality: As you bring your heart to God, he will place his desire in you to such an extent that your desire becomes his for you. So when you pray about a longing, and the desire remains, you can trust that God has left that in place for a reason.

It is a maddeningly mysterious process, really. Some desires God fulfills in spades. Others he transforms. And some remain like ladies-in-waiting, leaving a sad and tender ache for the time when you will know their total satisfaction—not here, but in heaven. I sometimes remind myself that God is not a vending machine where I put in my coins, and out pops the Pepsi. He is far less predictable than that. But he is utterly, utterly faithful.

Nothing about this journey of desire, though, makes much sense while you are sitting in the stands. God meets his friends on the field. Every time. Always in that place where you risk your heart. How he enters that game with you is the best adventure novel you will ever read, only it's your own life and you are actually living it! The only guarantees he makes are the important ones—the eternal ones. He has promised to bring us home.

What he asks of us is to stay on the field with him and to resist the urge to crawl back into the stands. In that hope, our longings are our best friends.

To live as a child of God is to live with love and hope and growth, but it is also to live with longing, with aching for a fullness of love that is never quite within our grasp. To claim our rightful place in destiny, we must not only accept and claim the sweetly painful incompleteness within ourselves, but also affirm it with all our hearts. To state it directly, *we must come to love our longing.* (emphasis mine)[12]

Exploring the question of desire is a necessary part of discovering what it is to be a strong woman with a soft heart. Given that we live on the far side of Eden and that this world will always fall short, desire will lead to pain as often as pleasure. And pain is a subject all its own.

How we see pain determines, in large part, the life of our hearts.

Listen with Your Heart

1. What kind of longings are stirred in you when you watch a beautiful sunset, or enjoy coffee with a good friend, or see a couple in love, or sit down with family over a holiday dinner? In what ways do you see those longings as a longing for God?

2. Think about C. S. Lewis's claim that when we wholly belong to the Lord we are more ourselves than ever before. How does that statement make you feel? How would your life be different if you more deeply believed that?

3. What would be different in your life if you trusted your redeemed heart more often?

4. What do you do on the inside to deaden yourself to desire? Do you see your desires and longings as too human, too selfish, too irrelevant, or too _____?

5. Isaiah likens desire to the condition of thirst. Read Isaiah 55:1–3. What does he encourage you to do with desire?

6. What does Isaiah say is the outcome of letting our desire lead us to God?

7. Think of something that you are overly attached to—perhaps food or a person or an activity of some sort. What are you after, really? What do you really want?

8. In Psalm 63:1–5, David considers the Lord the focus of his truest desire. Try writing his words in your words.

9. Is there any one area of your life where you sense God stirring in your heart to move you out of the stands and onto the playing field? What would give you the courage to listen and respond?

3

PAIN:
The Crossroads of the Heart

So much is distilled in our tears . . . not the least of which is wisdom in living life. I have learned that if you follow your tears, you will find your heart. And if you find your heart, you will find what is dear to God. And if you find what is dear to God, you will find the answer to how you should live your life.

KEN GIRE

Indeed, the LORD will comfort Zion;
He will comfort all her waste places.
And her wilderness He will make like Eden,
And her desert like the garden of the LORD.

ISAIAH 51:3

As soon as my daughter stepped out of the car, I knew she was in love. It was like her eyes had been wired for lights. She had called the night before to say she would not be alone when she picked me up at the airport, and here she was, beau in tow. I watched as he tossed my suitcases into his trunk as easily as the footballs he had carried into college end zones, and I smiled. *Thanks for picking me up at the airport. So, you work for one of the engineering firms in the research park? No, I've already eaten on the plane.* I doubt even my best attempts at small talk could disguise that I was looking this guy over—as only a mother can.

My first thought was half-conscious, pure instinct: *This man is just too beautiful.* Faint blinking lights, innate female radar, warned me to beware a man so drop-dead gorgeous he could always have his pick. Some lessons in life you never quite forget.

But Allison did not have the kind of protective coating that comes with time and experience. What woman does at the tender age of twenty?

She went out, every night, with this gorgeous man. She was gone in more ways than one, actually. He made her feel like the most wonderful woman in the world, she said. They could talk for hours, absolutely hours, and never run out of things to say. They prayed together. She had never felt this way about a guy. And that was true; her heart had never been so engaged. Not like this, anyway.

I had misgivings I could hardly name. I kept hearing the lines of sad love poetry in my head:

When I was one and twenty, I heard a wise man say,
"Give crowns and pounds and guineas but not your heart away." . . .
The heart out of the bosom was never given in vain;
'Tis paid with sighs a plenty and sold for endless rue
And I am two-and-twenty,
And oh, 'tis true, 'tis true.[1]

I did not want my daughter to live out the same story of young and unrequited love. So I did, I think, what most mothers do. I tried to pray more than I actually spoke—which is to say that my prayer life was thriving. And I remembered, as if it had been yesterday, all the raw, tender vulnerability of falling for someone and hoping with all your being that he felt the same way.

Occasionally, I would venture a gentle note of caution. "You might want to slow this down, honey, see some other guys, let him wonder a bit," I told her. I even left a copy of *The Rules* on her nightstand—her generation's not-so-gentle guide to navigating the dating scene. But then I would look at her and think what it felt like to be in love for the first time. And my words, of course, were just muffled, babbling sounds in the background of love's warm café, where live music played night and day.

I awoke one morning to see her sitting at the foot of my bed, ashen-faced, waiting to tell me news I knew without words was not going to be good. "It's happened, Mom," she said.

"What's happened?" My stomach knotted with dread.

"I brought this guy to a new singles group in town he said he'd like to visit with me. And for two hours I watched girls swarm around him like he was fish bait that glowed in the dark. One of them is older, about his age—from his home state, a flirty southerner with a drawl that drips magnolia. And I can tell, Mom, he's starting to pick up with her."

I had some hope that she was just overreacting; a little too vigilant, perhaps. But as the weeks went by, her instincts proved true. Maybe they should just be friends, he said. After all, you are a few years younger than me. The gorgeous man began to pull away.

In the end, I was thankful I had prayed. Only God can mend the brokenhearted. Myself, being merely the mother in the picture, I offered the simple timeless soothers women use to staunch a female wound—a bit of shopping, a movie, a day at the beach. But how would this pain shape my daughter's life? That lay in her domain and God's. I knew, only, that I had a daughter with a broken heart.

How this pain would shape my daughter's heart was, indeed, a huge question. For I realized, from my own life and from the lives of women I knew, that we don't always come through such experiences for the better. I had visions of my daughter at thirty, steel in her eyes, still swearing the last thing she needed was a man in her life. It happens all the time. *I got burned . . . and I will not go near that stove again.* Whether it's the loss of a love or heartache from a hundred other sources, many a woman has had to work her way back from a frozen ledge.

THE FACES OF PAIN

Pain—emotional pain—is a curious thing. It takes place on an invisible level, yet it has the potential to actually shape the real stuff of a person's future. It can numb and destroy our passion in life, but it can refine and bless as well. When you're hurting, no amount of logic or rational thought will make it go away. It's almost impossible to make pain a mental exercise. And willing the pain to be gone—we've all tried that. *I will not feel this way.* It doesn't work too well, does it?

Artists say that nothing pierces the heart like beauty and pain. Not the stuff we acquire or the goals we accomplish. Nothing impacts us where we actually feel life but beauty—and pain. Pain is experienced as a wave, and the question is: How will we ride it so that we emerge in a stronger place, more grounded in God, more open to life, more wise?

Before we go there, though, it's worth looking at some of the shapes and packages in which we encounter the pain of life—heart pain—for it appears in our lives in many forms.

The Sudden

The Book of Proverbs speaks of "sudden fear" as a thing to be avoided. I used to wonder why. It is true that when loss hits in a quick way, there is no time to prepare. You are blindsided, caught off-guard. It's like skiing down a Colorado slope, on your merry way, and being clipped from behind by another skier. You lie on the ground for a minute, struggling to get your breath and wondering what hit you. Sudden pain—when life hits hard—is just like that.

I think of my friend who took one of those business trips with her husband, to a place where someone has tried very hard to slice up a piece of paradise and serve it to you. They are out riding bikes in the January sunshine of Arizona, having left a thriving business and two children back in snowy Minnesota. This is their time to get away and recoup. They are riding only a half a mile down a quiet street back to their hotel. And in an instant—just long enough for my friend to turn her head—a car driven by an elderly man on prescription pain killers collides with her husband, knocking him up onto the windshield of the car before he hits the pavement. An emergency helicopter air-flights him to the nearest hospital.

Life happens. And none of it catches God by surprise.

My friend is grateful that her husband even lived through the experience. But when they walked out of the hospital two weeks later, she sensed that her husband was not exactly the same man, different in ways it would take months to assess.

Now, four years later, their lives have taken a course neither would have expected in their wildest dreams. Her husband's personality changes remain—some for the better, others not so good. He has cut back on his work in significant ways. As a couple, they have begun to major on one thing they always did well—parenting. In addition to their own two, they have adopted four Russian children and their house thrives, but in such different ways than it had before.

Sometimes when my friend and I talk, we recap the ways her life has changed. And we always come back to the same point—the suddenness of it all. Her life was heading one way, and in an instant, just long enough to hear the crash of metal, her life embarked on a new course. She rode a wave of pain—a staggering amount of loss and change and gutsy trust—to get to this new place.

Some of the pain that comes into our lives is just like this—out of the blue, totally unexpected, mind-boggling. Life is what happens to you while you were busy making other plans, John Lennon once said. That is true—life happens. And none of it catches God by surprise. It may take us a while, though, to catch our breath, to ride the wave, and to trust that God has something in mind—something good—that we would never have dreamed.

The Subtle

Other pain is less tangible and harder to name. It's more like a dull toothache that sticks around too long. We would hesitate to complain. But even pain in its subtler forms shapes the heart, and as such, deserves attention.

When our children were small, my husband was invited to begin a leadership institute that was part of a Christian conference center, a place designed so that participants could study, grow spiritually, and work in the same location. It was a great dream. It was also a dream we felt God had called us to, so we packed up home and hearth and moved three states farther west to follow it. For four years we worked—hard. We gave it all we had and then some. Only by degrees could we admit to each other the hard facts: The dream wasn't working as planned. Work and study and spiritual growth on the same small premises was a bit too much for everyone concerned. We were burning out. Maybe God had called us there for reasons other than "the dream."

During that time I found myself watching the same film over and over, somehow captivated by the story line. *Out of Africa* is the movie version of Isak Dinesen's poignant tale, which begins with the words, "I had a farm in Africa . . ." Basically, it is the story of the events that led to the heroine owning a coffee farm in Africa then falling in love—and how that dream shattered around her. It's a lovely, heart-rending story. I would watch *Out of Africa*, grab for a Kleenex at the end, and then a few days later, watch the movie again. I was flat running out of Kleenex.

I slowly realized that I was drawn to the film because of the parallel with my own life. I was feeling similar disappointment over the loss of a dream. The pain involved was so subtle, yet so persistent, that I could not name it for days. And when I could, I no longer needed to see the movie.

We don't usually connect the experience of emotional pain with losses so much a part of the flow of life. Sometimes, things just don't work out. You take your lumps and get on with it—at least that's what you tell yourself. But the life of the heart doesn't really work that way. God did not mean for it to. Even the subtle forms of pain—the loss of a dream, the loss of an old identity, the loss of a valued ability—need some space to be acknowledged. If we just skip past, we miss more than we realize. How can we pray over something we cannot name? How does God meet us when we don't know where we are?

The Amplified

Sometimes, when I sit and listen to women tell their stories, I am amazed at how a childhood wound will repeat itself in an adult life in almost uncanny ways. And when this happens, the pain is not simple pain. It's amplified in some way, like pain squared.

The first time I met Laura, she had been separated from her husband for months. He had taken up with a woman in his office, claiming he was bored. He needed a change in his life. Laura handled the situation as well as any woman could. She had her own disappointment to consider, and the pain of two teenage children as well.

The hardest part, she finally admitted, was that her father had left her mother for another woman when Laura was about the age of her own daughter. So every time she saw her daughter's distraught face, she remembered the old pain of her own father's adultery—and the present reality of her husband's. She felt in stereo, so to speak, experiencing the past and the present at the same time.

This kind of situation is not that unusual. Individuals who have experienced an early and profound loss—like the loss of a parent—tend to lay all future losses in the same grave. It's a place they have been before. The terrain is all too familiar.

There is a measure of surprising and merciful grace in amplified pain, though. God often allows us to be wounded in the same location of an old wound. The pain—in his hands—has an antiseptic quality, with the potential to cleanse and make new. The right steps we take in the present, the words we speak that have always needed to be spoken, tend to touch both places in our lives simultaneously. What we do to deal with the past affects the present; any change in the present also helps to heal the past. It's a bit like a two-for-one special, well disguised.

FACING YOUR VULNERABILITY

OK . . . so the pain you encounter in life can take many shapes and forms.

It is almost impossible to get through life intact, unharmed, untouched. I sometimes think of a character in the novel *White Oleander* in this regard, an adolescent girl who had been shuffled from one foster home to another. She looked at other kids her age who still had their innocence, who had not been touched by pain—yet. "To them," she said, "pain is a country they have heard of, maybe watched a show about on TV, but one whose stamp has not yet been made in their passports."[2]

What a thought—the idea that somehow we meander through

life, and somewhere along the way, pain enters our lives and leaves an indelible mark, as though it has actually been stamped on our passports.

My point is that eventually pain does get stamped on your passport. No matter how hard you work to avoid it, pain makes its appearance; and the hardest part to accept, sometimes, is its inevitability. Often when a woman seeks help from a friend or a counselor, what she's saying is, "This pain, this terrible thing wasn't supposed to happen. Tell me how to make this go away." And it's hard to sit there, knowing that what she is slowly coming to terms with is the practical reality of a theology she has always known: This is a fallen world and some part of that ruin has invaded her life. She is vulnerable.

I had this mental image of how my life should be. . . . And try as I might, I could not get reality to match the dream.

The whole notion that some part of the pain of life is unavoidable is not an easy idea to confront. Especially for Christians. We tend to see our lives as a series of hurdles, which, if we trust God and jump high enough, we can get through without scraping our knees. If we miss a hurdle, though—or come through bloody and bruised—we must have done it wrong. We have failed in some way. Or worse, God has failed us.

It is a strange fallacy for a people whose faith includes a cross and whose Savior agonized in a garden over the suffering he was about to face. But it is an illusion that is, nonetheless, hard to shake.

I think it took me almost the whole decade of my thirties to accept the unavoidable aspect of pain—the gap between what seemed meant to be and what was. I had this mental image of how my life should be, a painting on the wall of my mind. And try as I might, I could not get reality to match the dream. So much I had expected to happen didn't, and the wild and unexpected seemed to appear on the scene regularly and unannounced. I wandered around, a little bewildered. Should I go to graduate school? Would our son ever struggle less in school? Would my husband find the truly right expression for his gifts and dreams? Maybe it was more Bible study or another self-help book or seminar I was missing. I kept searching for the key to make the picture come together in one beautiful whole. And I could not—just could not—find it.

Now as I listen to other women and reflect, I realize that most of us have a time in life like that. The decade of the thirties, for instance, is notorious indeed for the way it butts us up against the pain and challenge of life and then asks us what we are going to do with it. The illusion of immunity evaporates. *This was not supposed to happen to me—but it has. My husband has left for another woman. My child continues to struggle. My illness can be managed, maybe—but not cured.* We come up against something that will not yield, despite our best efforts. We make peace with the pain of life.

One of my favorite southern novelists claims that you know you're an adult when you start to realize that some sorrows in life will never go away. You learn to carry them with you in ways that enrich rather than debilitate your life, in ways that make you wise. But the dark and knubby places in the fabric, the tapestry of your life, remain.

Somehow, I know she is right.

THE INVISIBLE FORK IN THE ROAD

It's not enough, though, to accept that some brush with pain is inevitable. If it were, all we could say is one big, "Oh, well. That's life."

But there is more—much more—and so I return to the story of my daughter with the broken heart. I admit that I wondered exactly where Allison would go with the loss of this love. I had visions of triumph, hope that she would just let this be his problem and go on.

And I had a few nightmares of what this could look like if bitterness and resignation took up residence in this wound. In the end, I would have to say that my daughter followed her heart, which is to say that she took some time to catch her breath and cry her tears. She resisted the temptation of "If only." If only I were prettier, thinner . . . whatever. What is not is simply not meant to be. She prayed. And slowly, she edged her way into the hardest part—daring to trust again.

This process I watched in Allison I have confronted a hundred times in myself and with other women. It can be summarized in a single question: What will you do with your heart? You can play the game of pretend. Or you can get stuck in the dark and ugly, wrapping yourself in the strangely warm cocoon of anger and bitterness. You can take all the longing of your heart, so exposed in this loss, and determine you will not hurt like this again . . . ever. Whatever course you choose, your heart knows the truth: You have come to an invisible fork in the road.

What I really want most to say is that it matters where you go from here. It matters to you and to everyone you love. It matters to God. For the secret you stumble on is that if, once hurt, you open your heart and let God take you by the hand, he will lead you to a better place than you have known. Not necessarily easier, but a place of freedom and even joy.

Pain is the special province of the heart. And in the providence of a merciful God, he is able to convert it to something golden. Something good.

There are inevitable losses in life. But there is one thing you do not have to lose—your heart. Some tragedies can't be prevented. But that tragedy can. In the next chapter we will continue to look at the life of the heart in the hope that, indeed, the prospect of losing heart does not describe your life—or mine.

Listen with Your Heart

1. If you think of pain in terms of loss or failure or real disappointment, then through what significant experiences has pain entered your life?

2. What experiences have been the hardest to deal with? Why?

3. In what way has a painful experience in the present amplified something from the past?

4. Job said that man is born to pain as surely as sparks fly upward (Job 5:7). At what point in your life have you come to see some measure of pain as an inevitable part of living in a fallen world? How did your perspective on life change as a result?

5. Some pain enters our lives due to our own sin. Can you describe a time in your life when the pain you experienced was due to a wrong choice? How does Hebrews 12:5–7 encourage you?

6. Isaiah describes the pain of life in poetic terms—as a desert, a wilderness. What is the promise of his words in Isaiah 51:3?

7. If pain represents an invisible crossroads, what would motivate you to walk through the experience with God, determined to keep an open heart?

4

LOSING HEART:
How It Happens

Thus we become strangers to ourselves, people who have an address but we are never home and hence can never be addressed by the true voice of love.

HENRI NOUWEN

The other gods were strong, but Thou wast weak.
They rode, but Thou didst stumble to a throne;
But to our wounds, only God's wounds can speak
And not a god has wounds but Thou alone.

EDWARD SHILLITO

Years ago, when people wore bell-bottoms the first time, there was a little paperback book passed from hand to hand in Christian circles. Written by an obscure missionary in Palestine, *Hinds' Feet on High Places* captured in pure allegory the heart of following Christ, much as *Pilgrim's Progress* had in another generation and time. The basis for the story is rooted in a beautiful Old Testament image that Habakkuk uses—the idea that God is taking us to the high places, where we will be able to walk as surefooted as a gazelle along the narrow edges of a cliff through the difficult places of life.[1]

The main character is a shepherdess named Much Afraid. She comes from "the family of the Fearlings," but her biggest problem is that she is lame in both feet. The Shepherd has promised to take her to the High Places, though, and so she sets out, lame feet and all. She has only to follow the Chief Shepherd. Her journey is strangely captivating.

At one point, Much Afraid is utterly perplexed that the Good Shepherd has provided two companions to accompany her whose names are Sorrow and Suffering—of all things. Much Afraid's response is a little too familiar. She pleads with the Good Shepherd. "I can't go with them. I can't . . . why do you do this to me? It is more than I can bear. You tell me that the mountain way itself is so steep and difficult that I cannot climb it alone. Then why, oh why, must you make Sorrow and Suffering my companions?"[2]

As a young woman fairly new on this spiritual journey myself, I read those words and thought that was a great question! The idea of being accompanied by Sorrow and Suffering as I followed Christ was a bit of a shock at first. I had missed that in the fine print of the brochure, so to speak.

I can still remember the sense of hope I felt when I got to the end of the book and watched Much Afraid discover that as she accepted these strange companions their names were changed to Joy and Peace. They became her guides; they shaped her soul. It was my first inkling of a bedrock principle of the heart: If you want to know real joy in life, then be willing to let pain tutor your soul.

Passion in life is comprised mostly of the stuff that comes from the tutoring process—slowly and mysteriously—like a phoenix rising from the ashes of despair. I should add that the root of this word *passion* gives us significant clues as to how we acquire it. It means "to suffer." It's as though some wise old soul was trying to let us in on a little secret. *So . . . you are interested in the passionate life. You want the real thing. Are you willing, then, to grapple with a bit of pain?*

Passion is a two-sided coin on which joy is wedded, inextricably, to sorrow, and wisdom is purchased at the feet of suffering. You won't know many moments of being Cinderella at the ball without sweeping up your own pile of ashes and cinders. The real prizes are never cheap.

Proverbs encourages us to watch over our hearts carefully because all the wellsprings of life flow from this place.[3] The laughter and love and courage and sacrifice that make life worth living are born here, in the inner world of your deep heart. God means for you to have access to that world. It is the incubator of your passion for him, the essence of the real you. It's the place where you can be at home with him in the truest sense of the word.

So losing heart is a serious matter, one that is worthy of real thought on our part. It takes a variety of shapes and forms.

PLAYING IT SAFE

I mentioned in the first chapter how easily we get cordoned off into the little rooms of our lives. We make a commitment to play it safe. What feels safe, in an emotional sense, is what others seem to want of us—and after a while, that becomes the only self we offer the world. Frederick Buechner put this especially well:

This is the story of all our lives . . . and in the process of living out that story, [our] original shimmering self gets buried so deep that most of us end up hardly living out of it at all. Instead we live out all the other selves which we are constantly putting on and taking off like coats and hats against the world's weather.

[If we continue] we run the risk of losing track of who we truly and fully are and little by little come to accept instead the highly edited version which we put forth in hope that the world will find it more acceptable than the real thing.[4]

Our original shimmering selves get buried deep, and we live out of all the other selves, which we put on and take off as need be, like too many wraps on a cold day. What a great image. Can you identify with his words? Do you occasionally get a glimpse of the woman you know you are, deep down? Can you feel the temptation to bury that and to offer instead an edited version of yourself that seems more what others want?

Isn't this one of the truest stories of our lives?

In many ways, this story is as old as Adam, as familiar as his response when God came looking for him. "I was afraid . . . so I hid myself," Adam said.[5] We have been echoing those words ever since. It's the story of all our lives: In our fear, we hide. Desperate for a more presentable self, we grab what fig leaves we can to meet the world as we find it.

For if there is a higher opinion and it really matters, and God values what we are prone to throw away, then we can live out of the whole of who we are under his blessing.

I remember talking with a young woman, very artistic by nature, but driven and unable to relax enough to make much of her creativity. Cheryl was so-o-o tired. The demands of two children and a home and a part-time job kept her running. But really, it was more than a busy family. She longed to sit down and read a book or get out her box of watercolors. But there was no permission inside her for that. Her sensitive, creative self was something to be held at arm's length and indulged only if everything was done. Which, of course, it never was.

When I see something so inviting in someone—so genuinely *them*—I always wonder where that got pushed aside along the way. And so I asked Cheryl, "When did you decide this sensitivity, this creativity, had to be kept under lock and key?"

Cheryl related the story of growing up as the shadow of her

dentist father. She followed him around, hoping to be invited into his confidence, but she could never find much of a place in his life. Cheryl wanted something from him he didn't feel he had to give. After a hard day of talking to teeth, he craved solitude, and his study was his sanctuary. And so they danced, father and daughter, always at arm's length, never quite in step, missing each other's cues.

Her dad complained that Cheryl was too sensitive. He felt that her feelings were too easily hurt. Her creativity was a waste of time. After a while she began to see her sensitivity as a problem. All her efforts were thrown into becoming the star student, which she did, and the softer parts of her soul were stuffed somewhere out of the way.

I offered the thought that, perhaps, sensitivity seemed to her to be the thing that kept her from having a relationship with her father. So she tried to dispense with it. She nodded her head.

"How do you think God sees your sensitivity? How does he feel about that part of your soul?" I asked.

This is the hinge, in each of us, where our stories turn. For if there is a higher opinion and it really matters, and God values what we are prone to throw away, then we can live out of the whole of who we are under his blessing. We do not have to bury huge parts of our hearts. In Cheryl's life, the needed permission to get off the treadmill of doing so much was found in the very sensitivity and creativity God has given her. Now there is more of a sense of God's pleasure in the simple things of her life—reading a book, painting, enjoying her children.

In a rather humorous way, author Anne Lamott likens a wound to the spirit to a wound to the body. She tells the story of having her tonsils out. The first time she tried to swallow after the operation left her clutching her throat in agony. Time to call the nurse. Lamott was hoping for serious pain medication, but the nurse encouraged her to chew gum, vigorously. And swallow! Apparently a wound to the body causes the nearby muscles to cramp around the wound, protecting it from further injury. Those muscles must be used again for the cramping to relax and the pain to go away. Lamott says,

> I think that something similar happens with our psychic muscles. They cramp around our wounds—the pain from our childhood, the losses and disappointments of adulthood, the humiliations suffered in both—to keep us from getting hurt in the same place again, to keep foreign substances out. So those wounds never get the chance to heal. . . . They keep us standing back or backing away from life, keep us from experiencing life in a naked and immediate way.[6]

That's a great analogy. The healing of the heart happens in a similar fashion. We have to do the thing we cannot do, as Eleanor Roosevelt once said, the thing that makes us grab our throat and take a deep breath. Maybe it's starting to name our real feelings and share them with someone who may not always receive them well. Or embracing the discipline we need to walk with God, not knowing what doors that will open. Or refusing to run away from conflict because that has always seemed easier than facing it.

In the healing of heart and body, the same paradox is at work: If you step into the pain, you find it lessens. The screaming wound is slowly transformed into an old scar—more sensitive to the touch, perhaps, but the ache is dulled and occasional. The fear does not control you.

It turns out that playing it safe, at least in matters of the heart, is the most dangerous thing you can do. By that route, you become a butterfly pinned to the wall, with wonderful colors and all kinds of potential but going nowhere. Your wings are clipped. To really fly you must claim the courage to live out of your real self, the one God called into being.

POURING ACID ON HOPE

When my husband and I traveled to Russia, we ran across a Russian proverb that arose in the days of Stalin, when so many lives were lost and dreams died: "The tallest blade of grass is the first mowed down." That was a Russian means of encouraging people not to stand out in any way. It was better to melt into the crowd. Don't try to change things. The best chance for survival lay in the giving up of hope. Sixty years later, when the Berlin Wall came down, outsiders discovered a sea of defeated people—men, especially—who had been taught from their earliest days not to hope. Hope could bring a swift end to your life.

In a similar sense, pouring acid on hope is one way we get stuck in the emotional place of lost heart. It's very logical, in a strange sort of way. If we can talk ourselves out of hoping, then the pangs of disappointment will miss us too. Or so it seems. As one writer says, "Hope is by far one of the most dangerous commitments we make in life."[7]

When I am dulled to hope, I can sweep a lot under the rug-of-doesn't-matter.

Pouring acid on hope is a sad dynamic in anyone's life—human and logical, but deadly. I think of a woman so frustrated by the unfaithfulness of her husband that when he left, she would ride around listening to romantic music on the radio, saying to herself over and over, "Suc-ker. What a sucker you were for ever loving that man." As though the key to not hurting is to kick yourself so hard you can't feel anything.

I can still picture a penitent husband who confessed his affair with deep regret and turned to his wife in the hope of working hard to salvage their marriage. The response he got chilled my bones. "Oh, you don't love me," she said. "I know you—you just want some other woman." As though she could prevent the pain of being abandoned again by becoming the one who pushed away.

I see myself, pretending I have no expectations so I don't have to grapple with the loss of something. It doesn't matter if what I write actually gets published. Catching up with my husband after one of his long trips is not all that important. When I am dulled to hope, I can sweep a lot under the rug-of-doesn't-matter.

Oh, the games we play with ourselves.

I once heard an older, seasoned therapist say that the hardest thing for him in helping people is to watch the profound human tendency we have to sabotage ourselves. We are afraid to hope because we might encounter loss, so we nip it in the bud. Something we have always wanted can be right at our fingertips, right in our laps, and we throw it away. It's like watching some dark force at work. We can be right on top of something for which we have worked and prayed, but then we run for the hills when things get difficult. Like the woman who insisted her adulterous husband couldn't possibly love her, we close the door on our own fingers.

We literally push away life when we push away hope.

Eventually, this tendency to sabotage ourselves leads to a distorted view of God. It seems as though God is the one who is cold and withholding. That may be true of an alcoholic parent, it may even be true of ourselves. But it is not true of God. If it seems that way, we are projecting someone else's face onto God. "For of His fulness we have all received, and grace upon grace," John said.[8] In other words, God is endlessly giving. He will give us what we truly need in his time. But if we have managed to douse hope, we will be the last to know it.

If we do not let ourselves hope in God, we will turn in another direction, sometimes without knowing it. By default, we will depend on ourselves. We will put our hope in people, often the wrong people. The picture is not a pretty one. In an effort to wake us up, God offers some of the strongest words of warning against this very human tendency to lean in the wrong direction, to "make flesh our strength":

> Cursed is the man who trusts in mankind
> And makes flesh his strength. . . .
> For he will be like a bush in the desert
> And will not see when prosperity comes,
> But will live in stony wastes in the wilderness,
> A land of salt without inhabitant.[9]

In this bleak picture, good things come into our lives, but we don't see them. We do not recognize prosperity when it comes—the shape and form of God's goodness set in the landscape of our individual stories. It's not the packaging we had in mind, and so we push it away.

Hope that is pinned to God, rather than to people, has a buoyancy to it because it is grounded not in our own illusion of how our story should read, but in the character of God. And so, your husband may indeed leave for another woman. The book may never be published. The business may never quite get off the ground. But we dare not let go of our hope. We stay alive to the possibility of encountering something really good, so that we can welcome it when it comes. We won't have our backs turned. As David wrote in the Psalms,

> I would have despaired unless I had believed that
> I would see the goodness of the LORD
> In the land of the living.[10]

David expected to see the goodness of God in his life—at any possible moment, in the most unlikely of situations, because good is simply how God is. A sense of expectancy rooted in the goodness of God keeps hope alive.

I often think of the story about George MacDonald, a Scottish writer from the last century who lived a remarkable life as the father of eleven children (many of whom he adopted) and the author of fifty-five volumes of fiction and nonfiction. Living in a day devoid of effective copyright law, MacDonald saw his work scandalously pirated. He died nearly penniless. But one of the last lines in his later works expresses the hope that kept his heart alive, through thick and thin. "A great—great—a great good is coming to thee," MacDonald wrote.[11] Hope sees God's goodness always right around the bend in the road.

MAKING A SILENT VOW

Perhaps you remember a scene in the movie *Gone with the Wind* in which Scarlett stands outside the ruins of Tara, a carrot in her hand and dirt on her face, and declares, "I will *never* go hungry again." She makes a vow. She will never again be in this place of poverty and need. Not while there is breath in her body. From that vow, Scarlet maneuvers her way into one of Atlanta's new postwar businesses—a steel magnolia of a woman, with emphasis on the steel.

Scarlett makes a good example because she provides a graphic picture of the kind of thing that takes place in all our hearts on some level—most often, in deeper regions where we are unaware. We live by inner statements that are born out of experienced pain, and these statements shape our lives more than we can possibly imagine. If the wound is great enough, or the experience happened early in our lives, these inner statements are much more akin to a vow. No way—not while there is still tea in China—will we get stuck in that experience again. That's the intensity associated with a vow. It's like concrete that hardens around a wound, something calcified that only the love of Christ can soften and dissolve.

Sometimes the vow is obvious and easily remembered. I met a

woman who was puzzled as to why she felt so little for her husband after twenty years of marriage. Granted, he had not been anybody's idea of a sterling husband in their early years. He worked too much—way too much. But he was trying hard now to salvage their relationship—offering love and attention in ways he never had before. And pretty much to no avail. Melissa was unmoved.

As we began to explore the early years of her marriage, when she was alone with most of the responsibility on her shoulders, we came across a moment when she actually remembered standing at the foot of her stairs and saying to herself, "I will not let myself need this man again." A small thing, perhaps, but a primary place where her heart made up its mind—and the shoulder she leaned on from that point on was solely her own. She could read every marriage book on the market, but her feelings for her husband would change only as she actively repented of the vow—as she was willing to risk letting herself need this man again.

> *We live by inner statements that are born out of experienced pain, and these statements shape our lives more than we can possibly imagine.*

Vows are so important because they set unseen forces in motion and our feet on a particular path, often without our knowing it. As Eldredge observes, there is usually a macabre sequence in this picture—a *wound* in our souls in which a *lie* takes up residence, from which a *vow* is born.[12] Rumbling around in the back of our minds, like steel barrels in a metal warehouse, are words like these: *I am on my own. The love I need will never be there.*

This sequence can happen early in life. The inner statements of our hearts are not complicated, but they are often buried deep; and like the templates on the ocean floor, even the smallest shifts will change all that lies above it. Those statements shape the way we see life—they determine what we are able and willing to risk of our hearts with others.

I remember working with a delightful woman in her early forties and feeling surprised to learn that her life had been the story of one bad man after another since she was fifteen years old. In two marriages and even with earlier boyfriends, Sarah had been a magnet for the man from whom she could expect nothing. She had never been able to break the pattern and had endured years of verbal abuse and addictive behavior from men, in order to enjoy the few brief interludes when things were good. And she had finally grown tired of simply enduring.

As we talked, the conversation turned back to the subject of her adoption as a small child. Sarah had no memory of her mother, but her adoptive parents had been wonderful people, and she loved them. "How did you see this thing of being adopted as you were growing up?" I asked her.

"Well, I assumed somehow that if I had been a lovable little girl, my mother would not have left me," Sarah replied. The *lie* that sets up in the *wound*.

"And how did this figure into the men in your life?" I asked again. "What did it seem a man could do for you that would heal the pain of your mother not being there?"

She had to think about that for a while. Then it came to her—like a bolt of lightning. "Why, it was a man who would take away this branding of not being lovable. A man would finally make me lovable." Here was an even deeper lie in the original wound. It's not hard to discover the vow that follows these lies: *I will find a man to love me and to make me lovable. I will. I will. I will.* The *vow* that is born from the *lie*. She had craved attention from men all her life, seeing it as the source of her emotional redemption. Being alone—without a man—meant she was no one. So she took whatever male attention was offered.

There is something about stating a vow plainly that allows a woman the chance to see through it. For as this woman realized, no man could validate her worth to that degree. No man could make her lovable. God is the One who has known her, and loved her, long before any human being came into the picture. In the sacrifice of his Son, God declared her lovable. Would she let herself receive what she had always wanted—the real thing—rather than settle for the paltry shreds of love she could find in human form?

Since lies have a way of masquerading as truth, and vows are not easily seen, how do you know when you have made a vow? There are at least two clues. One or both of these are often present around a vow, like smoke that indicates there is fire somewhere.

"I've been here many times before." The making of a vow generally leads to some kind of compulsive behavior—as Sarah had to have a man in her life, even if he did not treat her well. It's the definition of insanity: repeating the same poor choice over and over, each time expecting a different outcome. When there is a vow present, it feels as if you are locked in the same dance steps to some dissonant strain of music, that sheer will power does not seem to affect. To break the spell, ask yourself a few questions: What kind of pain am I trying so hard to avoid? What do I actually believe will bring me life?

"This feels like life and death." Often, in the smoke around an inner vow, there is a great deal of fear. The fear may not be rational, because strong inner statements or vows are formed not out of wisdom and trusting God, but on the basis of what seems like survival at the time. They may follow the line of your family's code—the accepted way by which love and approval were meted out. So, if you don't follow the yellow brick road, something terrible might happen. What are you afraid will happen to you if you don't . . . ? What will somehow be "true" about you if you don't . . . ? And how can you allow God to meet you in that fear?

BEING ABLE TO HEAR GOD

So here we have them—the cramped dark corners our hearts so easily run to when we encounter pain. Our commitment to playing it safe. The struggle to hold on to hope. The silent vows we make that lock our hearts in place.

But God refuses to leave us there. He comes calling, sometimes in strange disguise. Love comes calling—but not always as the comforter and protector we expect. God uses the pain of our lives like a surgeon's scalpel to open the very wounds where our hearts believed a lie. He exposes our real fears. He brings to the surface the deep convictions that have shaped the way we see ourselves—and the way we see him.

More than four hundred years ago, Saint John of the Cross wrote about this mysterious and unexpected way in which God draws our hearts to his. "God begins His greatest work when the inner man is opened to Him," John wrote. Then he added, "God will wound you deeply. For in this way, He continues to open all the inner chambers of your soul."[13]

Why would God go to such trouble—reaching into the farthest crevices of your soul, disturbing your plans, rattling your cage? Why not just leave you be?

Simply put, such disturbance marks your best chance of hearing his voice in the deep places where your heart makes up its mind. "In all this [wounding] God is opening the way to the central chamber of your soul. There He plans to set before you a feast. This, I tell you, is the banquet place of the Holy Spirit," John of the Cross explained.[14] Only when the heart can hear, can we receive the experience of being loved, the joy of belonging to the Father. And pain is often the megaphone that awakens.

In the inner chambers of your heart, God steps past all your talent and hard work—all that you would think he values. He goes straight for the messy, broken places in you because it's there that you can truly discover him. This is the way he frees your heart to love, to risk, to grab hold of life for the joy that's there.

You will find that encountering the pain of life with your eyes open, determined not to pretend, is as much an invitation to a journey as Much Afraid received before setting off for the High Places. Along the way you will encounter your fear of losing control and your need to trust—important subjects for any who would travel well.

Listen with Your Heart

1. Where in your life do you sense yourself holding back, playing it safe? Why?

2. Have you ever been aware of sabotaging yourself, pushing away an opportunity or relationship that really could be yours, because you were afraid? How do you feel about that now?

3. If we shut down inside we will not be able to trust God in any real measure, and our focus will turn to others or to what we can do for ourselves. Read more closely the description of the person who puts his confidence in human beings, as Jeremiah records in Jeremiah 17:5–6. What will be true of his life?

4. The person who puts his confidence in God is described in verses 7 and 8. What is true of his life?

5. Inner statements are borne of experienced pain, and they shape our lives in more ways than we can imagine. Think of places in your life that represent loss or pain. What are some of the false conclusions you may have drawn about God, about yourself, about life?

6. In this chapter, I wrote about how Sarah looked to men to prove she was lovable. Is there any way in which you identify with her? To what or to whom do you turn for validation? Why?

7. Read Psalm 51:6. What does this say to you about God's desire for your life?

5

CONTROL:
Releasing Our Sticky Fingers

Deciding what I most need out of life, carefully calculating my next move, and generally allowing my autonomous self to run amuck inflates my sense of self-importance and reduces the God of my incredible journey to the role of spectator on the sidelines. It is only the wisdom and perspective gleaned from an hour of silent prayer each morning that prevents me from running for CEO of the universe.

BRENNAN MANNING

It helps to resign as the controller of your fate. All that energy we expend to keep things running right is not what keeps things running right.

ANNE LAMOTT

On a morning just like every other morning of my life, I looked in the bathroom mirror to wash my face. Only on this morning, I noticed a small brown spot near my eye. *Strange spot for a freckle,* I thought. But then, I am a galaxy of those.

Only this freckle grew a bit—ever so slightly, hardly noticeable, but difficult to ignore since it was right next to the corner of my eye. So I had the dermatologist take a look—a knowledgeable older woman with enviable skin, who has led the state association of dermatology for years.

Not to worry, she said. I should come back every six months and let her examine me, but women do get freckles and sun spots and zany little markings as they get older. I toddled out of her office happily.

I came back every six months, as the responsible patient, for her to check my spot—which continued to grow. It grew by the tiniest of increments, but it grew. Maybe we could just—like—take this thing off my face, I gently suggested to the doctor. That was not a good idea. It's hard to tinker with skin around the eye, she said. Surgery is especially difficult, as it requires using a skin graft, and then you have to make your two eyes match. That would be important.

Just the thought of a knife near my eye made me weak in the knees. Yet this crazy brown spot stared me in the face every single morning. Finally, I asked her if we could biopsy this thing—for the curiosity of it and all—since it had been here for some time now.

She agreed to take a small nick out of it and send it off to the lab. "But I'll tell you frankly," she said, "there is not one chance in a hundred that this is skin cancer."

I was the one in a hundred.

Sometimes, now, when I look in the mirror at a grafted patch of skin about the size of a dime, unbelievably close to my right eye, I am reminded that I did not write the script for my life. (The surgeon, by the way, did a masterful job. He inherited nimble little fingers from his mother, a fine seamstress in Brooklyn.) But, really, how many times does a woman with brown hair and brown eyes get skin cancer at the age of forty-eight? And out of all the square inches of skin on my body, right beside my eye?

All of us want to hold on to the illusion that we are in control of our lives. At least a little bit, anyway. Especially if, basically, we've been good girls, and that sort of thing. There is nothing like a stray diagnosis—or any one of a hundred other unexpected happenings—to remind us that we are not in control.

But that doesn't keep us from trying.

Becoming a strong woman with a soft heart will, indeed, bring us face to face with the need to feel in control. Control is the most subtle of dynamics, as natural as the air you breathe. It's the insistence that your life follow a particular path. It's about having an agenda for your life—a picture of some ideal that is shaped, usually, in childhood. We tote it along through life, often blissfully unaware, until it dawns on us that IT'S NOT HAPPENING. Or at least not happening in the way we had hoped.

Perhaps you will identify with my friend's story as much as I did when she shared it with me. We were sitting outside a coffee shop one lovely fall day, the sun warming our backs as we consumed steaming cups of coffee and shared some of the unexpected turns our lives have taken. "You know what memory floats back to me every so often?" she said.

All of us want to hold on to the illusion that we are in control of our lives. At least a little bit, anyway.

It was the memory of a big weekend conference she had attended when she was in her early twenties, just after she began to follow Christ. At the end of the meeting everyone was asked to take out a blank sheet of paper and let that represent his or her life. They were to sign their names to the bottom of the blank sheets, as a way of offering their lives to God. She remembered praying, "Lord, you fill in the pages of my life. I have no idea what you've made me for and called me to. You write the story of my life."

For years she forgot that she had prayed that prayer. But illnesses and financial setbacks and broken relationships brought it back to mind, painful things she just had never envisioned in the script of her life. "I realize that my original sheet of paper was not so blank after all," she said. "Only now can I see what an agenda, what a set of expectations I've had."

I realize that *control* is a bit of a dirty word. We don't usually think in those terms. If someone stopped me on the street and asked if I had control issues in my life, I'd probably look over my shoulder to see if they were talking to the woman behind me. Who, me? In control? I haven't felt in control since the year before I had two children in diapers—some time ago.

What I am aware of, though, is this mirage that sits in the back of my brain. It appears more real at some times than at others. But in some form, it is always present, just off the wings of the stage. I call it the mirage of the genteel life. The picture is basically this: a family of beautiful achievers, no pain or sadness present, everyone getting along. I don't know why this mirage has such pull for me. Perhaps it's all the leftover fragments of girlish dreams tied up in a package. Simple things evoke it—the smell of magnolia in the spring, a table set with linens and silver—and I hear the siren call of perfect family.

Actually, my mirage is a lovely picture, but it is an illusion of paradise with my own monogram. It is an agenda. Sometimes it assumes idolatrous dimensions. How do I know that this mirage is more than a nice ideal and is, in fact, tinged with my own issues of control? Again, by simple things, like how hard I work to get the people I love to read off the same script. By the anger I felt when I realized I was the one in a hundred. By the disappointment I struggle with sometimes when it hits me that we are, even when we're cleaned up, a pretty ordinary lot. By the way I try to enlist God into making my version of paradise real, rather than submitting myself to the picture he has—which is always bigger than I can grasp.

Try as I may, I cannot make this mirage materialize. There is always some kind of brown spot in my life, staring me in the face.

I suspect that everyone has a mirage of some sort. A middle-aged man talked with me recently about his version—in male form, clearly. When he is traveling and tired, he said, it seems like the answer to his life would be a younger woman who wanted to have sex with him whenever he felt the desire. That would be life. He would be complete. He knows it's a mirage, but sometimes it takes a real conscious, prayerful effort to let it go.

We have our own personal versions of trying to arrange the pieces of life so that they make a beautiful whole—or at least keep things from getting worse. Often the mirages in our minds are not so much wrong—they're just *ours*. Our own agendas. The faces of control take such varied and subtle shapes.

Pam has a real gift of discernment and wisdom, and her friends seek her counsel often. She is a great listener—a real rock of a woman. What she can't do, though, is turn the tables and allow her own weakness to show. She feels exposed and out of control and sure that no one will really want her friendship on those terms. So she makes sure she stays the strong one.

Sarah has six months of freedom from alcohol, and she stands within reach of things she has always known God put it in her to do. So why doesn't she go for it, now that she's sober? Because she would succeed only too well, and she knows that too. Her life would be good—and she's not sure how to handle that. She feels in control only when she is half-alive—subdued and plain vanilla.

Vicki is married to a man with a chronic anger problem. She spends her life avoiding him because then, at least, she can stay clear of the criticism. It's a Catch-22, though, because he perceives himself as all the more unloved. And then he gets angry! Vicki feels trapped and depressed, because the only means she sees of avoiding his anger is to control the distance between them by running away from the relationship.

The need to feel in control is a subtle thing. Sometimes, as in the stories of these women, control has a benevolent face. However benign it looks, though, the need to control is really our passions turned neurotic. It usually takes one of two shapes. One looks anxious, overbearing, just plain trying too hard. The other is more a story of avoidance and self-protection. However control is expressed in your life, the important thing is to take stock of your own heart. What is the pain in your life that just sits there fermenting, expressing itself as control? And how would God lead you to deal with it differently, in a way that would express an active sense of trusting him?

Most often, our need to stay in control springs from inner vows we do not know we have made:

> I will not hurt like that again.
> I will never be loved the way I long to be.
> I am all I really have.

So, for instance, Vicki avoids her angry husband because he's too much like her father, and long ago she determined never to be hurt like that again. But her husband is a man she could appeal to much more successfully if she could let go and deal with her fear. Pam would find that her own concept of how to ensure love by being the strong one is flawed. What she sees as weakness looks to others like she's human and, therefore, might truly be a real friend. Control that springs from the vows we made in the face of pain truly clouds our perceptions.

Control masquerades as strength, but it's really not. It's more like teeth-gritting determination, or white-knuckled fear with an edge to it. We try to get a life by arranging the pieces as best our limited vision and wounded, misbegotten hearts can do. God may be a prop in the play, but he is not the director. Not really. Only surrender and trust allow him to take his rightful place. And the strength that comes from that—genuine strength—looks and feels different. It has more room for options, more freedom to reflect, more patience.

The effort to gain some semblance of control over life is as old as Adam and Eve. It's not a new invention. We are in familiar company, which is some consolation. When Adam and Eve lived in the Garden of Eden, there was an immediate connection between need and fulfillment. No lag time, so to speak. Outside the garden, though, where we live, is a different story. I suspect that if we could have eavesdropped on their conversation once outside the gates of paradise, we would have recognized their panic. *How will we ever live out here?* The bone-chilling reality must have set in for Adam and Eve, and they came to the same foolish conclusion we often do: They would have to make life happen as best they could on their own. The very essence of control.

Our predicament is that we must have life—and we cannot make it happen.[1] We long to be loved. We want our lives to matter in the scheme of things—and all these longings are legitimate. But we are hamstrung in really being able to bring this about in any significant or lasting way. My own mirage of the perfect family, for instance, can be turned upside down in a moment, as quickly as the screech of brakes that precedes a terrible car crash.

Where do we go from here?

FACING WHAT ISN'T WORKING

C. S. Lewis used a wonderfully helpful metaphor to describe the way we go about trying to construct our own image of life. He called it building "a house of cards."[2] We stack each piece on top of the other, carefully, hoping against hope that it will stay in place. The illusion never entirely evaporates that we can—if we try hard enough—actually get this thing to stand.

But always, always, always, some proverbial brown spot appears in the mirror. The business never gets off the ground. A child flunks out of college. The new husband has the oddest set of quirks. And the house of cards gets really wobbly—or it comes tumbling down. For a little while, at least, we see it clearly: This story is not going to work out according to the picture in our minds. It's simply a bigger story—and we didn't write it.

I can remember the time in my life when I first saw this clearly. I have a good friend from my college years who married an older man, a seasoned missionary. His first wife died and he had to raise four children alone for a few years. Having lived on three continents and seen a lot of life, he had been around, as they say. One night when I was visiting their home, the three of us sat up late after all the children had gone to bed, just talking about life. As I remember, I was moaning, in some discreet fashion, about the disillusionment I was feeling about the way a particularly cherished dream had fallen apart. I felt like God had really let me down.

Doug leaned over to me and spoke some of the wisest words of my life. "You have to realize, Paula, that your dreams aren't going to materialize in the way you have hoped—even the ones you thought God gave you. Some will turn out better than you could ever imagine. Some will go belly up. And hardly any will match the picture in your mind."

God gives some wonderful gifts in the here and now, but let's face it—they never really fill out the edges of the dreams we carry inside us.

Those were simple words, but so true, and they have returned to me a hundred times. *The ideal in my mind isn't going to work out in this life.* Much of the anxiety and depression women encounter seem to come from this reality. Perhaps the statement should be amended: It isn't going to work out in *this* life. God gives some wonderful gifts in the here and now, but let's face it—they never really fill out the edges of the dreams we carry inside us. The ache of incompleteness returns, a longing that is never truly satisfied. That can produce profound frustration with our lives and the people in them, or it can become the bread crumbs on the trail that lead to the beauty and wonder of being with the Lord in that great never-ending day. It will work out beyond our wildest dreams. Then. As Paul said,

> Eye has not seen, nor ear heard,
> Nor have entered into the heart of man
> The things which God has prepared for those who love Him.[3]

So we live with the paradox of longing amid incompleteness. "Our Father will refresh us with many pleasant inns on the journey," C. S. Lewis wrote, "but he would not encourage us to mistake them for home."[4]

The amazing thing is that God follows us into the blackened ruins of our failed dreams, our misbegotten mirages, into the house of cards that has collapsed on us in some way; and he speaks, not with the chastisement we feel we deserve, but of all things, with tenderness.

> "Therefore, behold, I will allure her,
> Bring her into the wilderness,
> And speak kindly to her.
> Then I will give her her vineyards from there,
> And the valley of Achor as a door of hope.
> And she will sing there as in the days of her youth,
> As in the day when she came up from the land of Egypt.
> And it will come about in that day," declares the LORD,
> "That you will call Me Ishi [husband]
> And will no longer call Me Baali [owner].[5]

Don't you find that when you offer to the Lord the crumpled mess of the dreams you can't make happen—of all you cannot control—what he gives you in its place is a mysterious sense of hope?

Out of the valley of Achor, which was a major scene of Israel's willfulness and sin, God resurrects hope by offering grace and mercy where none is deserved. And your relationship with him is different from this place. You serve much more out of gratitude than duty. God has your heart in a new way.

There is something wonderful in letting go. A. W. Tozer called it being released from "the fine threads of the self-life, the hyphenated sins of the human spirit," like self-sufficiency, self-pity, self-absorption, and self-hatred. Letting go means "freedom from the everlasting burden of always having to get our own way."[6] Having to stay in control, to get it our own way, is indeed an *everlasting* burden.

In recognizing the subtle stranglehold of control, in the release of my sticky fingers from the steering wheel, my heart is ready for the real adventure of life—actively trusting God.

Listen with Your Heart

1. If control is trying to arrange the pieces of your life into the picture you have in mind—trying to make life happen—then in what ways do you struggle with control?

2. What do you think makes it hard to recognize the dynamics of control in each of our lives? What kind of things do we mistake for control?

3. What kind of experiences, people, or situations make you feel out of control? What do you find fearful or threatening?

4. Isaiah presents one of the most descriptive analogies of self-will—control—in the Bible. He calls it kindling your own fire. Read Isaiah 50:11. What do you find sobering in this verse?

5. What is the contrast and the encouragement of the previous verse, Isaiah 50:10?

6. Think of your closest human relationship, the one you would most hate to lose. In what ways do you find yourself trying to control the relationship or what's happening between you? What are you afraid of?

7. What would it look like to trust God with the issues or relationship you are most tempted to try to control?

8. What would help you most to release your sticky fingers from the steering wheel of your life?

6

TRUST:
The Art of Falling Backward

The thing is to rely only on God. The time will come when you will regard all this misery as a small price to pay for having been brought to that dependence. Meanwhile, the trouble is that relying on God has to begin all over again every day as if nothing has yet been done.

C. S. LEWIS

It's a strange thing to discover you are loved when you know there is nothing in you for anybody but a parent or a God to love.

GRAHAM GREENE

*Surely I have composed and quieted my soul;
like a weaned child rests against his mother,
My soul is like a weaned child within me.*

PSALM 131:2

The best picture I have of what it means to trust came through a rather unusual experience—praying with a woman addicted to cocaine.

The circumstances were these: I came to work one day at the county drug and alcohol facility where I was serving a three-month internship. Almost immediately, the doctor in charge asked me to talk with a clearly distraught woman whose roommate had tried to commit suicide. "See if you can get her to calm down," he said.

So I sat with this tiny wisp of a woman in a steel gray room and heard her story. Sybil told me that, because of this addiction, she had lost everything in life that mattered to her—her three children, her marriage, her home. And now this. Her friend had tried to take her own life. She became more upset as she talked, and I quickly realized I had no words that could touch her. So I did something that is just not done in a county clinic—I asked her if I could pray for her.

"Oh, would you please?" Her openness surprised me. So I started to pray, something very simple. I have no memory of the words.

The woman before me, shaking and distraught, began to get very quiet—so peaceful, in fact, that I cocked one eye to see if she was OK. I finished praying. She was totally at rest.

We talked for a few minutes, and then honestly, I was caught so off-guard by the change in this woman's demeanor, I asked her what had happened as we prayed. What had she experienced?

I have never gotten over her response. Rather matter-of-factly, she said, "I saw God on his throne. And he asked me to sit in his lap. Then he said, 'There now, Sybil, you will be OK. *You will be OK.*'"

Whenever I am in search of this illusive thing called trust, I return to my memory of this comforted woman, as calm as a small child at her father's knee. I realize God is offering me the same place on his lap. The same door into trust is open to you and me.

Between your longings and the demand for their fulfillment is a place as real as any in the tangible world. But it is uncharted and uniquely tailored to your own personal story. You will only know you are there when you feel a little on the edge of your chair—and yet strangely at peace. Getting there, sometimes, feels like a miracle itself.

It is the place of trust.

Trust hangs somewhere between knowing what your heart longs for and trying to dictate the shape or timing or outcome of your heart's desire. It lies in the willingness to accept the particulars of how and when and where God chooses to intervene. It waits in the cool shade of surrender.

There are loads of things that lead us, if we let them, to trust God—things like losing our health or having a child or finding college tuition, or even the next breath. But I offer an illustration out of the world of relationships, because as women, relationships are central to our sense of well-being. And just as relationships elicit our deepest longings, so, too, trust can be more difficult when it comes to those we love.

When I met Carol, the thing she wanted most was her husband's attention. She organized her life around him, which he interpreted as clingy pressure. In his midforties and having met his professional goals, he seemed to be vaguely dissatisfied with nearly everything in his life. On some days, Carol was sure that included her. Her reaction was to just try harder. What did he want? Gourmet meals, better sex? The harder she tried to gain his attention and approval, the busier he stayed. Carol prayed that God would show her what to do.

Trust hangs somewhere between knowing what your heart longs for and trying to dictate the shape or timing or outcome of your heart's desire.

Carol grew tired of the emotional roller coaster she was riding. When her husband seemed happy, she was happy—at least for a brief time. But when he got cross with her, she could feel herself wilting like pansies in the hot sun. She was nobody, then, and it bothered her to see how much her identity was attached to his opinion of her. She felt like she was Velcroed to him—painfully stuck.

As we talked, Carol tried to find a way out of her predicament. "Maybe I need to become a Buddhist," she said, half-joking. Maybe that way she could detach from this object of attachment (which was her husband) and simply not care as much. She would be free, then, from wanting what it seemed she couldn't have. She would be able to stop trying so hard to make it happen.

What Carol is voicing here is how hard it is to live in a place of trust—somewhere between longing and demand. We tend to ricochet between two extremes, falling off one side of a horse only to get up and fall off the other. Sometimes a woman will admit it almost angers her to be in the presence of someone whose love and approval she wants, when it's clear that love eludes her. It cannot be guaranteed. Real love is like that, though. Real love can always be refused. It is sobering to realize how powerless you are to make someone love you.

Carol's journey of unsticking from her husband was a major foray into a new kind of trust. She began to deal, first, with the way she had attached her larger sense of being, her identity, not to God, but to a person. A human being, even one who is your husband, never makes a very good anchor. Carol had been accustomed to filling in the gaps of their conversation—their lives, really—with chatter and details and endless organizing, because she was afraid if she did nothing, their relationship would fall apart. Trusting God meant allowing those gaps to be there—letting go of her sense of control. Only an active transfer of her trust from her husband to God could allow Carol to love this man without making him the mirror of her worth.

So trust hangs out there in an open space, fluid, somewhere between these two poles of longing and demand. It is not detachment in the sense of resignation. We don't just throw up our hands and say, "Oh, well, guess I lost that one." Desire is still present, but there is an internal letting go of the focus of our attachments—a surrender of the particular means of trying to make our agendas happen.

THE ROOT OF TRUST

When you really want something, as Carol longed for her husband's approval, trust can seem like the rarest commodity in the world. It can't be learned in a class. You can't order trust from a catalog.

Trust does not come by working harder. If you've ever tried to conjure up a sense of trust, especially if you've been hurt or disappointed, you know how elusive trust can be. If you are frantically trying to hold on to something you think you just must have, then trust seems about as feasible as a Sunday stroll on Mars.

A major turning point in my life came when I realized that being able to trust God is grounded in staking the whole of my being on the reality that he loves me. I wonder, sometimes, whether trust comes by any other route. Friends may leave, my children may turn out to be reprobates, the mountains may crumble—but if I am loved by God, somehow it will lead toward the light. And apart from the reality that he loves me, trust is just wishful thinking— hopeless naíveté in the face of a cruel and capricious world.

What makes the Christian experience of surrender and trust unique is that when you let go of the object of your attachment, you are not shutting down on the inside. In experiencing the disappointment of a longing, you are accepting that loss as an invitation to a fuller experience of your heart's real desire—*to know, at the root of your being, that you are loved*. Disappointment is often the back door into grabbing hold of that reality more strongly.

When the future looks bleak, or someone has trampled on your heart with football cleats and you are struggling with trust, there is something gripping in the word *already*. You are *already* loved. Before the foundation of the world, in a way you can never earn, beyond the validation of any human being, you are loved. The essence of what we long for is already ours, in the truest sense. Disappointment drags us back to the well. Perhaps this is what the apostle Paul meant when he practically gushed about the length and breadth and height and depth of the love of God.[1] No matter how often you return there is more to be had. Always more to be had.

It helps, sometimes, to speak out loud, so you can hear them, the words the father spoke to his elder son in the parable of the prodigal: I have always loved you, and all that I have is yours.[2] God himself also speaks those words to us. *I have always loved you, and all that I have is yours.* They are profoundly reassuring. Slowly, mysteriously, trust takes root in you again—and your anxiety will ease. You will feel a little more like the weaned child of the Psalms.

I have a friend, Bob, who told me once about a morning he spent with the Lord and an unusual interaction that took place. Bob had wanted to get a better grasp of the love of God. Being a lawyer by trade, he put the question out there, straight up. He said, simply, "I need to know, Lord, if you really love me." And Bob waited— but the response that came to him was not what he had expected.

Letting ourselves be loved by God is the place where we stumble upon trust.

As clear as a bell, the words formed in his head. "Well, Bob, what do you think?" Bob sat there for a moment and then he agreed. "You're right, Lord. You do love me. I know you love me." It was as though God had been waiting for Bob to grab hold of that reality, not because it made it any more true, but because it made it his.

I find this such an accurate picture of the way God works in a person's life. We think some grand achievement or someone's approval will finally baptize us with the sense of being loved. But the need to trust is our invitation, over and over, to the place where we look into his face—and no one else's—and let ourselves be loved by him. *We let ourselves be loved by God.* Our hands release their grip on the reins of our lives and we stop trying so hard to be women with all the answers.

There is nothing on the planet quite like this freedom. I am sure this is the joy that sent Francis of Assisi dancing naked down the street. When you taste a measure of being able to love and enjoy the people in your life, without having to have any particular response from them, you are tasting bliss. You can move out into life, and you don't have to have your parking ticket stamped by human approval to do it. Letting ourselves be loved by God is the place where we stumble upon trust. It is the essence of one of the Old Testament's most engaging pictures of freedom:

> But for you who fear My name the sun of righteousness will rise with healing in its wings; and you will . . . skip about like calves from the stall.[3]

THE HAIRY NATURE OF TRUST

Having said all this about the need to trust and the fact that trust is rooted in being loved, I feel I should offer a disclaimer—a sharp dose of the reality of the struggle.

You probably have the same reaction to glib pronouncements about the need to "just trust God" that I do. When someone pats you on the back and says God always comes through, you have to wonder how well they know him. Are they taking into account how truly different the ways and means and timing of his coming through may be from what we have in mind? Are they acknowledging his unsearchable judgments and his unfathomable ways? I would be the last to imply that trust is an easy thing.

For almost four years we followed closely a good friend's battle with a brain tumor and his profound longing to stay in this world long enough to raise three young children with his wife, Pam. Great medical care and a lot of prayer brought Tim to a place where it seemed he just might make it for the long haul. There was real hope. His tumor had shrunk enough to allow a new treatment—a shunt placed in his head, delivering tiny injections of chemotherapy directly into the tumor itself.

Tim endured another surgery, but for some reason, the shunt placed in his head refused to seal. There was no medical remedy left to try. I will never forget talking with Pam the day after they learned this new procedure would not work for Tim—the utter, crushing disappointment of it all.

Tim began to go downhill rapidly, but about two weeks before he died, when he could no longer talk, he wrote out the last words he wanted to say to his wife and children. In his long and difficult battle with cancer, this is what Tim had learned—and what he wanted his family to remember. "The last words I want you to hear from me are that God is good, therefore my dying is good because he is in control."

The last words I want you to hear from me are that God is good— this is what the costly kind of trust looks like. I mean this reverently: If life is like a deck of cards, then God is always the wild card. He is not subject to our human efforts to influence outcomes. We are subject to his. His story is the great story being told—and none of us know exactly how our own story, set in this larger context, will read. Only that it will end well, ultimately. This is why trust, in the important matters, always feels like risk and why it entails courage.

To live with the Sacred is hard. It means that we walk with a God who does not explain himself to us. It means that we worship a God who is mysterious—too mysterious to fit our formulas for better living. It means that God is not our best friend, our secret lover or our alter ego. It even means that it is just as frightening as it is delightful to stand in his presence. Our creaturely relationship with God is one in which we are, at the same time, both irresistibly drawn to him and humbled by the grandeur of his holiness.[4]

Indeed, any serious grappling with trust will lead us to the heart of mystery, of all that God chooses not to tell us. And mystery, as someone once said, is an embarrassment to the modern mind. We find it hard to live with mystery. I once worked with a mother in the throes of grief over the sudden and inexplicable suicide of her daughter. There had to be a reason for this irrational act, something that would make sense of the nonsensical. "I think I know why this happened," she said to me finally one day. "This is God's discipline in my life. I know it."

My mouth fell on the floor. God's discipline? Through the suicidal death of her daughter? "That can't be," I told her. "It simply can't be. That explanation defies the heart of God." And then I realized what was happening to her. She was struggling to accept the mystery of something she would never know—and sometimes that can be terribly hard to do. It's much easier to blame ourselves or to blame others. But accepting the mystery of what we cannot know will lead us to the heart of God where we trade our craving for explanation for a simple willingness to trust.

THE ART OF FALLING BACKWARD

So having acknowledged that it takes genuine courage to trust God, what does trust look like? How does it feel? Let me offer an image from a group exercise in team building because I believe the analogy is an accurate one.

Here is the picture: You are standing with your teammates at the base of a ladder that has been leaned up against a tree. Your job is to climb the ladder, then fall backward into the interlocked arms of people who, in most cases, you have known for only twenty-four hours. You are unable to see their arms outstretched as you fall. You can't check their grip to make sure it's secure. You take a deep breath and let go, falling backward for what seems like hours. And then—just as you think you will surely hit the ground with a thud—you are caught and held and set upright on your feet once again. It's wonderful—after you get past the shock.

I find the actual experience of trusting God in the realm of my heart's longings to be roughly analogous to falling backward through thin air without being able to see how I will be caught.

There is a great story regarding trust from Mother Teresa's life. It seems that a young man sorely needed direction in his life, so he traveled to Calcutta to spend three months at Mother Teresa's mission. On the first morning he met with her, she asked what she could pray for him.

"Pray that I would have clarity," he said.

Mother Teresa replied firmly, "No, I will not do that. Clarity is the last thing you are clinging to and must let go of." When the young man commented that she always seemed to have the clarity he longed for, she laughed. "I have never had clarity; what I have always had is trust. So I will pray that you trust God."[5]

The real need is not clarity, as we think, but to be able to trust. The path will always appear no clearer than one little step at a time.

The struggle to trust is hardest in the face of sharp loss. Dale Hanson Bourke wrote of the wrenching experience of carrying twins, one of whom died in the womb. As a mother, she encountered death and life at the same time. She says,

When Tyler was finally born and I began to heal physically and emotionally, I still felt lost spiritually. At that point I feared that I would become bitter and closed off. So my simple request to God was, "Keep me open." I had no idea what it meant, but I can see now that it must have been music to God's ears. For the first time in my life, I had no preconceived notions of how God worked or how he would change things so they would go the way I had planned. *I was simply laying my life out for him to work as he saw fit. I was, for the first time, willing to be prepared instead of in control.* (emphasis mine)[6]

Deep grief has a blinding quality, and it can easily seem at such a time that God is nowhere to be found. We cannot trace his hand in the dark. We discover later, around the bend, that he has been there all along. Writes Brennan Manning, "The scandal of God's silence in the most heartbreaking hours of our journey is perceived in retrospect as veiled tender Presence and a passage into pure trust that is not at the mercy of the response it receives."[7] What seems like God's silence can be the gateway into a trust that is not dependent on circumstances—one that trusts on a basis deeper than what is seen.

When I am struggling to trust I find an old Quaker means of prayer especially helpful, because it is so concrete. Sitting with hands open in your lap, the prayer is simply, "What you put in my hands, Lord, I will receive from you." Then you turn your palms over. "Whatever you take out of my hands, Lord, I will let go." It sounds childlike, but then isn't it usually the scared kid in us that finds it so hard to trust? The Quakers acknowledged prayer as a special means of coming to trust when the way is difficult. The need to control being the insidious thing it is, prayer acts like rock salt on winter ice, unthawing the heart a little at a time until, out of nowhere, come the actual stirrings of trust we can feel.

The real need is not clarity, as we think, but to be able to trust.

Often, prayer precedes trust—and not the other way around. In my daughter's senior year of high school, she came down with mysterious stomach problems from a parasite she had contracted the summer before on a trip to Russia. We live between two university medical centers, but after the best help to be gained from both, six months into more medical tests and remedies than I could count, Allison was still losing weight and experiencing round-the-clock pain. I fought the frequent urge to panic with prayer. So much so, that I began to talk to God in shorthand: "It's me, again. Same thing.

Allison is getting worse. I'm really scared. Help." I felt like the widow knocking on the judge's door, over and over.

After a while, I was sorely tempted to not pray. Nothing was changing in this picture, except that Allison was getting sicker. But I could sense God drawing me. There was a new kind of bond being built between us. I was not learning to trust as I prayed; it was more like I was being given trust, as though someone were knitting little pieces of golden thread into my heart. *Whatever happens, I can trust you.* In the prayer in which I thought nothing was happening, quite a lot was happening in me. It took almost another year of various remedies before Allison was back to normal.

If we return to the analogy of trust as the experience of falling backward and discovering you are somehow mysteriously held, then the question you might legitimately ask is, What exactly am I falling backward into? It's not thin air or the arms of other people or the cushions of your own self-effort, but the goodness of God. *Trust is allowing yourself to fall backward into the goodness of God.*

Oswald Chambers noted that doubting whether God is really good and has our best interests at heart is the deepest vulnerability of our soul. Is God really good—in the face of all there is to lose in this life, all the longings that won't be realized until heaven? I mean, really? That was the challenge Satan snared Eve with—and her bite into the forbidden fruit was her vote to the negative. Curtis and Eldredge write,

> The question that lingers from the fall of Satan and the fall of man remains: Will anyone trust the great heart of the Father, or will we shrink back in faithless fear?[8]

We drop anchor in the goodness of God. The psalmist said that we should give God thanks and praise his name for one main reason: The Lord is good. David ended his most familiar psalm with the same focus. "Surely goodness and mercy shall follow me all the days of my life: and I will dwell in the house of the LORD for ever."[9] The literal translation is even better: Surely goodness and mercy will *pursue* me all the days of my life. The imagery in this verse is that of a highway patrolman who tracks you down with lights flashing and siren wailing—not to give you a ticket, but to give you a taste of his goodness and mercy. Writes John Piper, "When things are going 'bad' that does not mean God has stopped doing good. It means he is shifting things around to get them in place for more good. . . . He works all things together for good for those who love him."[10]

Your trust and willingness to take your sticky fingers off the steering wheel of your life rest on the risk that, in fact, the goodness of God will catch you when you let go. What you don't know—and why the risk feels electrically charged—is how and when and in what manner you will experience his mercy. You are simply and mightily assured that you will.

And that is how it is that you can be on the edge of your chair— and yet strangely, at peace.

Listen with Your Heart

1. Trust hangs somewhere between your longing or desire and the realization of that longing—between desire and demand. What makes trust hard for you?

2. Have you ever lived through Carol's experience, where you tried to make another human being your anchor or a mirror of your worth? What happened to the relationship? What happened to your sense of worth?

3. Proverbs 3:5–6 (NKJV) gives some of the Bible's simplest and most profound encouragement about trusting God. It says: "Trust in the LORD with all your heart, and lean not on your own understanding; in all your ways acknowledge Him, and He shall direct your paths." How would you describe "trust" from these verses?

4. What does the phrase "letting yourself be loved by God" mean to you?

5. What is the connection you sense between being able to trust God and knowing you are loved, profoundly, by him?

6. What would it look like to trust God with some of your bigger fears? How would your life be different?

7. There is a wonderful progression of thought in Psalm 116:1–7 that grounds trust in the character of God. How would you put these verses in your own words? In what way do they bring hope?

WINDOWS INTO
THE HEART

7

VULNERABILITY:
The Secret Side of Strength

What language shall I borrow to thank Thee, dearest friend,
For this Thy dying sorrow, Thy pity without end?
O make me Thine forever; and, should I fainting be,
Lord, let me never, never outlive my love for Thee!
— PAUL GERHARDT, 12TH CENTURY

My flesh and my heart may fail,
But God is the strength of my heart and my portion forever.
PSALM 73:26

When we think about being strong women, there is one version that we rarely consider. It's an awesome kind of strength, and there is really no way to be a truly strong woman without it. It is the strength of vulnerability.

I am speaking of that paradoxical place where you discover the strength God has placed in you by actually risking the pain you would normally run from—especially in close relationships. You step into the difficult place and find you are not blown away. Hearing a friend's criticism, you resist being defensive. You take the humble road, and find that it is the means of walking straight and tall. You say the words you need to say. In these kinds of moments, you can almost feel your soul expand.

Family holidays can be a real trial when two sisters can't get along. Judy and Lee had been at odds for longer than most of the family could remember. Judy found their estrangement especially difficult to bear. As little girls Judy and Lee had been quite close, playing happily for hours. When they entered their teenage years, though, and their parents divorced, the rivalry began— and it never went away. They competed over grades and boyfriends, and by the time high school was over, they hardly spoke to each other.

Judy was never sure why. She made a few halfhearted efforts to patch things up, but the coldness continued. Lee had been known to spread rumors about Judy in the family that were untrue, yet hard to successfully defend. So Judy just kept a safe distance. Holidays became superficial events, uncomfortable for the whole family. But no one knew how to unthaw the ice.

As Judy began to think about her life, she realized that the pattern of her relationship with her sister spilled over in many ways. She had not made many close friends—she found it hard to trust people. She didn't see herself as a woman that other women would really want to know. Judy felt there was nothing that could be done to change things with her sister—but the truth was, she had never much tried. Thoughts of encountering her sister's anger made Judy quickly tuck tail and run.

But as Judy's spiritual life deepened, talking with her sister seemed less impossible. She could sense it was a risk God wanted her to take—to really put her heart out there and ask if there was some way to pick up together in a new place.

Maybe Lee would continue to be the ice queen. But at least Judy would have broken out of the passive, silent place she'd lived so much of her life.

Have you ever had an "impossible person" in your life, with whom most of your interactions inevitably led to rejection and hurt feelings? If so, then you know the courage it takes to risk your heart—to be vulnerable—and to love in the face of that. That courage, exercised wisely, is like lifting weights in a gym, except that the strength you gain is an inner one.

In many ways, vulnerability is the last thing we would expect to combine with strength. The word literally means "able to be wounded," and therefore, vulnerability flies in the face of our usual concept of strength, certainly the one served up to us daily. To be vulnerable is to voluntarily place yourself, for the sake of a larger purpose, in a situation that could bring pain. You see something at stake—your own spiritual growth or someone else's—and you are willing to risk your heart in a vulnerable way.

I should add that the model of strength that is worshiped in our culture is the kind of power that prides itself on shielding from pain. It is quite different. The strong women who peer at us from magazine covers and movies are steel magnolias, lovely to look at, but impenetrable. Their charisma is designed to render them immune to the possibility of being hurt. In our culture, women worth their salt are too self-sufficient to actually feel real

> *To be vulnerable is to voluntarily place yourself, for the sake of a larger purpose, in a situation that could bring pain.*

gaping needs in their lives. As Simon and Garfunkel sang, a strong woman could pass for the rock that feels no pain and the island that never cries.

The Bible also speaks of being a strong woman—though clearly, another version. "Who can find a virtuous woman?" Proverbs asks.[1] The word for virtuous is *hayil,* a Hebrew power term used to describe robust things like amassing an army or the strength of a horse. "At each stage of a woman's journey . . . strength is her defining attribute," Cynthia and Robert Hicks write in their book about the biblical stages of a woman's life.[2] To be a strong woman is a worthy goal. Solomon devotes a significant portion of his book on wisdom to spelling out the qualities of a strong and virtuous woman. Whatever Christian stereotypes we may have built of female strength as pink and passive and empty-headed do not square with Scripture.

The strength God would shape in us, though, is vastly different from the kind with which we are confronted each day. We really have no purely human model for it. To see strength fleshed out in breathtakingly vulnerable terms, we must look to God himself.

THE VULNERABILITY OF JESUS

Until the time of Christ, the whole idea of being a god meant having the power to be above the suffering of human existence—to be immune from pain. That's what gods did. They remained impassive, above it all. A pantheon of Greek gods looked down from their perches upon the foibles of mere humans. Freedom from suffering was what defined being a god. Power made them invulnerable. It's not unlike our modern notions of success and being number one.

Imagine, then, what a radical departure from this picture the life of Jesus was—what God does with his power is so different! Christ, who created the world, allows himself the indignities of being a baby. The One who leads the stars out at night, as Isaiah wrote, permits himself to be crucified between two common thieves. The first public words ever spoken of Jesus address him not as King—but as the Lamb who takes away the sin of the world. Behold the Lamb! There is no more vulnerable animal. God exercises strength, all right—but not in the manner we are used to seeing.

The God who loves in freedom is not afraid and therefore can risk vulnerability, absorb the full horror of another's pain without self-destruction. God has the power to be compassionate without fear. . . . God's power looks not like imperious Caesar but like Jesus on the cross.[3]

Our most cherished notions of success and strength bite the dust before the reality of a God who makes himself known in his vulnerability—clinging neither to beauty nor honor nor power.

In our own lives, there is no way to escape a measure of pain—it is unavoidable. By the very nature of things, we are vulnerable. With Jesus, it was a different story. At every juncture, he could have removed himself, or taken the easy path. And he did not. *His was a chosen vulnerability.* He stepped into the drama he created and took the very worst part, the Hero who bore the spit and scourging of people he had come to save.

There are glimpses in the Gospels of the vulnerability Jesus chose that make you catch your breath when you think about them. How, in the Garden of Gethsemane before his death, Jesus asked his friends to stay awake with him. God of very God, in the moment of his anguish, voiced the longing for companionship. Or the tender way Jesus asked Peter after his great failure, "Do you love me?" Can you imagine Buddha or Mohammed asking his followers if they really loved him? As Brennan Manning once said, no other world deity ever stooped to voice such a question.[4]

This turns our notion of strength upside down and on its head. If God does not use his power to remove himself from suffering or pain, then vulnerability becomes a hallowed thing. It takes great courage to be a strong woman with a soft heart—but it is possible in Christ. It is the model of strength he lived. And the gift of that to us, in practical terms, is that we do not have to go through life using all our energy to hide our hearts and protect ourselves. We can walk into the fire of a difficult conflict or situation and not be consumed.

We can love others with real abandon. We can trust a God who has nail prints in his hands.

DISCOVERING YOUR HEART

The sort of strength that Jesus modeled—and that God offers us—opens up a world of possibilities when it comes to our own hearts. For the heart is the seat of our deepest sensitivities. It's the place we can feel most trampled upon—and where we don the steel-toed shoes that trample others. Any real spiritual transformation begins here. And yet, as strange as it sounds, attending to our own hearts is often what we are most likely to skip over.

I sat in on a fascinating discussion at a recent women's retreat that crystallized for me the way women feel about their lives. How do I manage it all? they asked each other. So many people need something important from them—children, aging parents, neighbors and people at work, a husband. They felt forced to choose. What got lost in the equation was often themselves—the "I" in the midst of the "we."

Women have this unique ability to compartmentalize their lives—it's a real strength. Family. Friends. Children. Husband. Work. Church. It's the way we keep things going smoothly, like air-traffic controllers making sure all the planes land and take off on time. There is one little compartment, though, we tend to leave out—our own selves. Or to change the metaphor, many woman feel they have to take a ticket and stand in the back of the line, and if there is anything left over, it's theirs.

Although, of course, we would never treat a good friend like that.

Sometimes we don't have a category for our *selves,* and so the whole idea of discovering our hearts seems foreign. Or selfish. Or hopelessly introspective. *What do I really feel about this situation? What do I think? Where do I sense God in it all?* But vulnerability and strength are like all personal growth—they happen from the inside out. God has set it up that way. As Moses said,

> Give heed to yourself and keep your soul diligently, lest you forget the things which your eyes have seen, and lest they depart from your heart all the days of your life.[5]

We begin with our own hearts—and what God is saying to us. We don't just skip over our dreams and fears and needs and losses. We listen to God in the midst of them.

There is permission, not to be self-centered, but to count yourself in the picture. All real ability to genuinely offer your heart to others—which is the essence of vulnerable strength—starts in this place. I know it sounds like a paradox, but you can't really love other people well unless you are at home in your own soul. You will simply be too afraid.

You can't really love other people well unless you are at home in your own soul. You will simply be too afraid.

I will never forget the words of a friend, a busy pastor's wife, as she described a wrenching period in her life after her father's sudden, tragic death. She said, "I took some time to wade through the grief and confusion—to feel the impact of my father's death. I wanted a soul that I could walk around in." In the best sense of the word, she was giving heed to herself by slowing down long enough to feel the impact of significant loss. She was taking the time to know her own heart.

When I open my bathroom cabinet, I find myself staring at this vast collection of creams and potions I use to take a few years off my face. So much time and attention goes to the external stuff. It makes me think: *Am I giving this much attention to my inner life, to my own heart?* Or do I expect that to just take care of itself, like God would wave a magic wand over me? I would like, someday, to feel that my heart has matured and that my insides actually match the maturity of the wrinkles on my face.

Discovering your heart is heavily dependent on reflective processes—most of which take a little time and attention. But they pay big dividends, all out of proportion to the effort actually invested. A little pondering goes a long way. A little pondering is also the natural accompaniment to prayer.

Journaling

Even if you only pick up paper and pencil when something is needling you, journaling pays some of the richest returns in discovering your heart. "How else can we learn about ourselves if not by forcing our hands to tell the truth about our hearts?" Nicole Johnson writes. [6] It is incredible to see the way feelings and conclusions you did not know you even had slip out the end of a pencil. Then you know much more how to pray. Journaling is like a farmer tilling the soil—only this is the earth of your life that's being tilled. The seeds of truth sink in much deeper, and God shapes wisdom in your heart.

> Thou dost desire truth in the innermost being,
> And in the hidden part Thou wilt make me know wisdom. [7]

Perhaps you feel intimidated by a blank sheet of paper. Let me encourage you that journaling is not like any other kind of writing you ever do. It's not an essay or anything that has to look polished. In journaling, you don't think so hard. You just take an open-ended sentence like, "What's bothering me about this situation is . . ." and you begin to write. And you write and write until all your feelings and thoughts are spent. It helps to write out the worst of how you're feeling—all the crummy parts you hope no one ever finds, the embarrassing-to-read stuff. Then ask God to give you some insight and begin to write again—only this time, write the reassuring truths you sense God would say to you in the place where you're stuck. Some call this "the trip in and the trip out," and it is a way of actually experiencing God's work in you.

Journaling is about the best and cheapest therapy there is. As C. S. Lewis once wrote, "Whenever you are fed up with life, start writing: ink is the great cure for all human ills, as I have found out long ago."[8]

I have been amazed at the personal insight and inner freedom women often gain through writing—especially when the writing consists of words they have long needed to say, but for some reason could not. A woman came to me who had been forced to put her mother in a nursing home, where she lived only a few months, drifting in and out of consciousness. A nursing home had been one of her mother's biggest fears—and her daughter had carried twenty years of guilt in having to make that decision. So she wrote her mom a letter (shortened here for the sake of space).

Dear Mom,

I never got the chance to explain to you how hard it was for me to let you enter a nursing home when you were so sick. I know it was your worst fear come true. I felt so bad about it—for years, really. But it was the only thing that could be done. There was no way to care for your condition at home then—just no way. I knew if you had been in your regular mind, you would have understood what I had to do. You know I loved you. I always will. But I can't carry this guilt any longer and I know you wouldn't want me to. I did the best I could, really.

She says that as she was writing, it came to her: "My mother would have understood my situation. It's OK. I can let this go." She finished the letter in a different place than she started.

Writing someone a letter you don't send is the next best thing to having them sitting right there. It feels as though they are present. There is often an almost tangible sense of release in creating a context in which you can say words that have long needed to be said.

Solitude

If journaling is about taking time to reflect, then solitude means allowing yourself a little space to be. Whether it's a few hours or a few days, being alone has a medicinal effect—even for extroverts. Some of the most active, contributing women I know find a retreat center a couple of times a year—and they retreat from it all overnight or for a couple of days. Alone. Without a phone in their rooms. With no real agenda. They may walk and pray or take a long nap or journal uninterrupted or read the Bible. It's amazing how rich the options seem when there is nothing pressing you.

Solitude is like a tonic that tastes a little strange at first, but then, after a while, begins to soothe the soul. "In solitude I get rid of my scaffolding," Henri Nouwen once wrote.[9] There are no friends, no meetings to attend, no stuff to entertain—all the things we use to convince ourselves we are somebody. It's just us—and God. The great gift of solitude is in seeing that as enough. Solitude takes the toxicity out of being alone—and since feeling alone is often what we most avoid, that can be incredibly helpful.

SHARING YOUR HEART

Knowing your heart is only part of the story, though. The real test of vulnerability comes in the midst of relationship, in the presence of those we love and those we hope to be loved by. It comes in sharing our hearts with others.

When our children were small, occasionally I would see in their faces something so transparent it was like seeing clear through to the soul. Brady and I used to play a game when he was just verbal enough to have discovered the concept of "mine." I would reach down and grab one of his favorite Matchbox cars and say, "Mine." Of course, he was aghast. "No, mine," he would insist as he grabbed the car back and put it in his stash.

I would pick up his car again. Back and forth we'd go, playing this game until at some unforeseen moment I would scoop up Brady in my arms and twirl him around. "Mine. You're mine, Brady. You belong to me," I would say. His chubby little face would turn electric, radiating the pure and unfeigned pleasure of being wanted. Of belonging to someone. I knew when I looked at Brady in those moments I was looking through a window into my own heart—into every human heart.

As we grow up, we learn to hide all that—sometimes, way too much. It seems impossible that someone could really know us, with all that means, and still love us. You learn that the risk of rejection is real when you allow yourself to be known, when you share your heart with someone who matters to you.

Maybe this scene describes a place you've been. You are having coffee with a woman you would like to get to know better. The conversation lumbers along. You have covered all the familiar territory. You are vaguely caught up on all the surface stuff that is happening. And then it crosses your mind, the thought of confiding something about your life that isn't going so well—a failure, a struggle, a knotty place where you feel a bit crazy. And you take a deep breath and hold it. What if she looks at you as if you are just that—a bit crazy? And she implies, gently, that smart people don't have those kinds of problems?

What do you do with your heart when you've shared it?

Vulnerability entails actual risk—it's not a wimpy thing. Yet without it, we lead a pretty lonely life, holding our breath, rarely offering much of our selves to others. As T. S. Eliot wrote, we go about our lives "preparing a face to meet the faces that we meet."[10] Buechner explains it this way:

> [We] tell what costs [us] least to tell and what will gain [us] most; and to tell the story of who we really are, and of the battle between light and dark, between belief and unbelief, between sin and grace that is waged within us all, costs plenty and may not gain us anything we're afraid, but an uneasy silence and a fishy stare.[11]

Vulnerability means stepping into the uneasy silence and past the fear of the fishy stare, believing that God means for us to have real relationships in his Body. It is as we "walk in the light," where he is, that we have actual connection with each other.[12]

The question becomes, How much of your real life—your story—have you shared with people you care about? How often have you taken the risk to share your heart, to let yourself be known?

One aspect of sharing your heart that tends to be more difficult than others is allowing yourself to voice a need. Popular mythology says that strong women make it, basically, on their own. Independence and being able to do it all are the hallmarks of strength. There is

The truth is that none of us can do the superwoman thing all that long before the edges start to fray.

more than a little shame attached to the places in our lives where the myth of self-sufficiency implodes and our needs show through. God forbid that someone might perceive us as weak. Needs are often treated like roaches in a woman's emotional life.

I remember working with a woman whose husband was busy running for various political offices. It was like some unspoken pact between them that he would relate to the public and she would handle everything at home. And she did handle it for a number of years. She was the soul of efficiency. Except that she began to notice that she had the second glass of wine on occasions where she had resolutely stuck to one. And she felt lonely almost all the time. And other men caught her eye, when she used to hardly notice them.

"You know, God hasn't made you to be able to live like that," I gently challenged her. "The needs in your life that only your husband can fulfill—what are you doing with those?"

"I hate to think of myself that way," she replied. "Needing someone like that makes me feel weak—like there's something wrong with me."

I wanted to jump right out of my chair and shout, "There is nothing wrong with you!" But then I remembered how I've struggled with that. The truth is that none of us can do the superwoman thing all that long before the edges start to fray. Our humanity bleeds through.

It is essentially a worldly goal to live without a sense of need. And it's an illusion that all those needs can be met in this life. Needs are not enemies to conquer, they are part of what keeps us returning to the Lord. They form the essence of our connection to each other. God could have made Eve out of another pile of dust, but he took a rib from Adam's side so that ever after we might have the sneaking suspicion that something is missing without each other. To own your need of someone tells them that they matter. As Craig Barnes explains,

> In their created limitations, Adam and Eve were held together in a bond of naked vulnerability. . . . That is because in God's design we do not manage our needs, we confess them. Intimacy demands hearing and telling the truth, and it assumes that some pain will always be the cost of that naked vulnerability. Intimacy also recognizes that we will be inadequate to respond to the needs that are shared. *We don't mend each other's brokenness,* we just hold it tightly. (emphasis mine)[13]

That image of holding each other's brokenness helps greatly. It comes as a surprise to many women that there is actually a great deal of genuine pleasure in allowing yourself to enjoy needing someone. It feels right and good to let go of the myth of being an island—even when others don't manage to come through in all the ways you'd hoped. We don't mend each other's brokenness, we admit our needs and let that draw us to each other and to God. Which is just what having needs was designed to do.

HONORING YOUR HEART

Now for the harder part.

It's a great experience to share something important and personal with someone who matters to you—and lo and behold, they understand. They get it. It's wonderful when you can put your heart out there in some way and it's not trampled upon. Or you take a deep breath and actually ask for help—and there's a willing response. Or you put everything you have into an important project and it takes off beautifully.

Occasionally, it happens just like that. Wonders never cease. There is nothing so refreshing as the cool clear waters of validation.

But, sometimes, it's a very different story. And then what do you do? What do you do with your heart when you've taken a risk and it all falls flat? You get the fishy stare and no one says they understand—instead they imply that you belong on another planet, far away from them and all the truly good people. You share your heart in some way and you are anything but validated.

First of all, let me encourage you that the awful feeling in the pit of your stomach has a name. It's a version of aloneness—as in alone-and-not-OK. It's a tiny brush with shame. The temptation is to turn the experience back on yourself: *I blew it again. I'm always messing things up. I'm just getting what I deserve.* Most of us never get around to identifying how or why we feel so bad. We just spend mountains of energy trying to keep it from ever happening again. It's such a potent feeling that many recovering alcoholics admit that they drank—primarily—to avoid this very experience, the toxic feeling of being left out. Invalidated. Rejected. *Alone.*

So you are not imagining things. A brush with shame makes any of us want to run for cover. This is what makes vulnerability, in the interpersonal sense, such a matter of courage and strength.

But strangely enough—and this is the surprising paradox—the important thing about vulnerable strength is not the response you meet when you risk your heart. For a long time, how others receive you *does* seem like the big deal. It seems like the point of it all. But that is truly an illusion. The response you get is always secondary, always the icing on the cake. As Judy discovered in the

Real success is measured only by the courage it takes to do and say what needs to be done or said.

impasse with her sister, Lee, real success is measured only by the courage it takes to do and say what needs to be done or said. Strength becomes the amount of vulnerability you can offer. What it comes down to, essentially, is this: What will *you* do with your heart, even if no one understands or offers validation? Will you honor your heart with the dignity God does—regardless of how you are met by others?

Perhaps the riskiest place for any of us is in our closest relationships—like one of those moments when something matters to you immensely, and you would so, so, so like your husband to understand. If only he could lean a little closer and say, "Honey, tell me a little more about what's bothering you." Or even, "I know what you mean. That was really a hard experience." Or something. A few words of empathy, a hug, a gentle reassurance that everything will work out. Something deep in you would breathe a sigh of relief.

Many women say that putting their heart out there like this, with someone they love, is the most naked, vulnerable experience that they know. Even more vulnerable than sex. So, of course, when a man does what men can sometimes do—offer advice, try to fix it quickly, or just miss the moment entirely—well, it's not a pretty sight.

When that happens in my life, I want to curl up in a fetal position for a week. And I am married to a good man, one who really tries to meet me. But he is a quiet German, a man who ponders, and in those moments when I share something that I would share with no one else and Stacy stares at it blankly and makes no reply, a dark little temptation floats past my visage. I can feel myself vowing that I will keep my heart to myself. I will build a moat around my castle and never lower the drawbridge again.

I have to make the loop back around to the place where I can comfort my own soul and remind myself that sharing my heart was, indeed, the right thing—the good thing for both of us—the God-honoring thing. I honor my own heart, and the sting of disappointment eases.

When I see women live a picture of vulnerable strength, it always awes me just a bit. I've watched a mother continue to love her son when he was determined to throw to the wind every belief and value she held dear, and I've seen him return. I've watched a wife offer her heart to her husband, time and time again, when all he could perceive in her need of him was a mirror of his own inadequacy. I know women who will put everything they have into worthy causes God has laid on their hearts, even when they know the only cheers they will hear will be those in heaven. The face of chosen vulnerability—for the sake of greater, godly gain—always moves me.

So the strength of vulnerability is a curious mixture of discovering your heart and sharing your real self, as best you can, with the people God has put in your life. You can't shut down on the inside without quelling the very passion that makes the journey worthwhile. Those walls around the heart take buckets of energy to maintain and God has better things for his children to do. When we close off our hearts, we dishonor him.

God bids us come into the vulnerable place his Son occupied where the power of his life was born out of fearless trust in his Father. God offers us a special kind of strength, one that is rooted and grounded in a reality that transcends ourselves. It is a place from which risk—and therefore, love—is actually possible.

The strength of vulnerability is the fire of a tender heart that forges steel in the soul. As difficult as it is to live with a vulnerable heart, it is far easier than camping out behind a facade. Jesus is the Lamb who conquers. He says,

Come to Me, all who are weary and heavy-laden, and I will give you rest. Take My yoke upon you, and learn from Me, for I am gentle and humble in heart; and you shall find rest for your souls. For My yoke is easy, and My load is light.[14]

Listen with Your Heart

1. Feeling vulnerable is usually something we are taught to avoid at all costs. Vulnerability is often equated with weakness or powerlessness, and so it illicits feelings of shame. Pick one experience where you felt vulnerable and write a bit about it. What did you find difficult in the experience?

2. Now read the experience of Christ in his chosen vulnerability. Isaiah 53:2–3 records part of his experience. What about this most touches you?

3. In Isaiah 50:5–9, Christ shares how that experience felt from his perspective. Where did he turn for help?

4. What strength do you see in Christ's vulnerability?

5. If you have practiced journaling or intentional experiences of being alone with God, what benefits has either or both brought you?

6. Sharing your heart with someone can be a risky venture, but it can also be the basis of a close bond with another person. When do you find that hardest? What do you look for in a friendship that makes that more feasible?

7. When do you treat your own needs like roaches to be gotten rid of? Why?

8. How would your thinking have to shift in order to have permission to have or share a need more freely with someone who matters to you?

9. What does the concept of "honoring your heart" mean to you?

10. How do you see vulnerability as a reflection of being a strong woman with a soft heart?

8

FORGIVENESS:
Experiencing a Heart Set Free

In old Savannah, I said, Savannah
The weather there is nice and warm . . .
They've got a gal there, a pretty gal there,
Who's colder than an arctic storm
Got a heart just like a stone
Even ice men leave her alone
They call her Hard-Hearted Hannah
"HARD-HEARTED HANNAH"

The weak can never forgive. Forgiveness is the attribute of the strong.
MAHATMA GANDHI

When my husband was in seminary, we developed some close friendships over pork and beans with other couples in the same predicament—challenging studies and no money. One couple, in particular, had it worse than all of us combined. With two sons under the age of three, Marnie, the wife, developed Hodgkin's disease. She entered treatment and it looked as though she would recover well. To the astonishment of everyone, though, her gifted husband, who was also president of his class, suddenly dropped out of seminary altogether. And within a few more months, he was gone. Marnie was left to pack up her life and her two small boys and return to the East Coast, where she had grown up.

Marnie was devastated, as you can imagine. Divorce had hardly been a word in her vocabulary. But here she was—a cancer survivor, a single mother with two young sons to raise—trying to make some sense of her life. Clearly, her husband had issues from his past he had never confronted, and in the pressure of their lives, he had snapped. But understanding helped only so much. Marnie was still left with the fallout of his choice to exit.

We continued to be friends through the years. I would call Marnie occasionally to ask how she was doing and to offer support. I remember a major turning point in her life, which, strangely enough, centered around a dream. She saw the lives of two women played out before her. One was vibrant, alive, and still hopeful. The other woman was a shriveled old crone, angry and bitter with life. It was such a horrible vision that Marnie woke from her dream saying these words over and over: "God, don't let me become bitter. Don't let me become bitter."

Marnie knew, I think, that the possibility of getting lost in bitterness was real for her. And so she worked—she prayed and hung in with the process—until she reached a place of true emotional freedom, where she could forgive and mean it. It took a while. She looks back on that as something of a small miracle, a gift from God. In the years since, Marnie has raised two wonderful young men who are wise beyond their years and deeply committed to Christ. She weathered two more battles with cancer. And recently, Marnie married again.

If you met her, you would know that Marnie became the woman she first saw in her dream—warm and strong and very wise. You would never guess that a man walked out on her years ago and left her with two small boys—she is so not a victim. She refused, by the grace of God, to let that experience define her life.

When it comes to a major battle of the heart—being willing to forgive—Marnie is an unsung hero. I have to say that in spite of the miles between us, I have learned a ton from her through the years about the necessity, the process, and the potential in forgiving well.

The impact of forgiving—or not forgiving—on the heart is a challenge to describe, because it's not a process you can actually see. We don't advertise the fact that we harbor something against someone who has hurt us. Sometimes we don't know it ourselves. The subtle little clues just slip out the sides of our lives—a harsher tone of voice, a polite coldness, a dinner invitation never sent. Or as in Marnie's situation, some wrongs are just so blatant, it feels entirely justifiable to hold a grudge until the day we die. Well, maybe not quite that long.

But you know what I mean.

Sometimes I try to picture what unforgiveness would look like in my heart if I could actually see its presence. I suspect it looks like cement. A dark, sticky cement that shuts down my heart, piece

We don't advertise the fact that we harbor something against someone who has hurt us. Sometimes we don't know it ourselves.

by little piece, and turns it into something as hard as stone. I am not aware this is happening, of course, because everything still works and I am still moving through life. But there is less of me to offer others, less of me that can really respond to God. My heart has shriveled in some hidden but very real way.

I have to say that the prospect of what will happen inside my soul if I don't forgive has become worse than the work entailed in letting go of the pain of being wronged. I think that could be called progress.

I am not exactly advocating that you and I forgive for purely personal reasons—though it's true that we are the greatest beneficiary. Forgiveness is first of all a theological issue. It's one of the laws of the universe, as God has set it up. If he is willing to forgive, in Christ, what you and I have done in the face of a holy God, then who are we to nurse a grievance? If he is willing to cancel my debt for millions of dollars, so to speak, then how can I demand payment from someone who owes me a couple of hundred by comparison?[1] Fundamentally, we forgive because in Christ, we have been forgiven. The arms that embrace us are wide enough to embrace those who hurt us—and those we have hurt as well.

When forgiveness becomes hard to do, sometimes that is one thing that will dissolve the hardness in my heart. I have been forgiven by a gracious God.

The lack of forgiveness does exact a staggering toll, though. It can shape your experience of life. It can ricochet through the generations of a family like a Ping-Pong ball down a tight hallway. It's worth looking at more closely.

First of all, being unable or unwilling to forgive means that you remain emotionally under the control of the person who wronged you. Which is a bit ironic, don't you think? Here you are, desperately wanting to break free from the pain of it all, but unforgiveness is like Brer Rabbit and the Tar Baby—everything under the sun sticks to it. *We ourselves* are stuck to it. A harbored wrong can control a life. It becomes what we feed off of, and we feel full—occasionally even happy in our misery—but we are full of awful stuff.

I once worked with a young woman who had become sexually involved with a married man who worked in her office. When his wife confronted him, he dropped his relationship at work like a bomb and turned cold and distant. The younger woman was humiliated. She retreated to the safety of her own quiet apartment for the next year. By the time I saw her, she had not been out socially in so many months she felt she wouldn't remember how to carry on a conversation. The power of unforgiveness is that strong. She could not forgive the man who had spurned her.

"How long are you willing to give this man that much power over your life?" I asked her.

She chewed on that question a while, then she said, "You know, it's really myself I can't forgive."

Isn't that what happens so often in our lives? Sometimes the hardest person to forgive in the picture is ourself. For this young woman, her year of hermitlike existence had been an act of penance, the self-punishing fruit of being unable to forgive either the man involved or herself.

Sometimes the lack of forgiveness gets camouflaged. In a group, it looks like the fog of confusion. The issues are obscured, and no one knows quite how to proceed. There's a climate of resistance. When the individuals involved get alone with each other and do the work of forgiveness, it's like someone turned on the lights, and suddenly, the next steps are easily seen. Literally, the air has been cleared.

A married couple with buried hurts and unforgiveness may carry on a running dialogue of snippy little comments, arguing and quibbling over dinky things. They think they just don't communicate well. But if someone scratches beneath the surface, it often becomes evident that there are major events and hurt feelings that got swept under the rug—not addressed and not forgiven. And the relationship breaks down, bit by bit, until no one can even remember how things got so heavy and tense.

I wonder, sometimes, if forgiveness is a tougher challenge for women than it is for men. We are not more stubborn, but often we are more deeply touched by relational pain. In Carol Gilligan's famous study of children in a schoolyard, you probably remember her discovery that boys solved their disagreements far more quickly than girls did, because they were determined to get back to the game. When girls fell out with each other, the game was over. They were so affected by the relational impasse that the game no longer had much meaning. This difference in the way we approach having our feelings hurt generally persists throughout life.

Perhaps you could say that women are more porous. Being hurt by someone we love and trust sinks in to a greater depth, and we don't brush that off like dandruff on our shoulders. The work of forgiveness is more work, and it must be done more often. It's especially a challenge if we have trouble admitting we are hurt or angry. The ability to disguise real anger is raised, sometimes, to the level of fine art, and it is hard for us to see that behind the fury of busy activity, or sugar-coated superficiality, or frosty attitude is enough anger to light a blowtorch. It was with good reason that Shakespeare said even hell had no fury like a woman scorned.

There is a very helpful concept from the world of family therapy that gives insight into the impact of unforgiveness in a family. It's called "cut-offs." The word is used to describe relationships in a family where two individuals cannot work through hurt and pain, so they cut off the relationship. You have probably seen this in some form, because it can happen in any family. Uncle Seth refused to have much to do with his son, Hank, because he wouldn't join his church—so he left his Civil War rifle to his nephew. Grandmother Bess was left out of the will, and she hasn't been to a family gathering in years. Two uncles had a dispute over land and they rarely speak—that kind of thing. Interestingly enough, one root of the word *bitterness* actually means "to cut," and in families where cut-offs are present, there is usually no small amount of bitterness.

Unfortunately, the practice of cutting off relationships tends to run in families. Like a family disease, harboring anger and unforgiveness becomes an accepted way to live. But it exacts a great cost. As Harriet Lerner wrote in her book *The Dance of Anger,*

> Keep in mind that people—like other growing things—do not hold up well in the long run when severed from their roots. If you are emotionally disconnected from family members, you will be more

intense and reactive in other relationships. An emotional cut-off with an important family member generates an underground anxiety that can pop up as anger somewhere else.[2]

It's worth remembering that some of the clearest words Christ ever spoke concerning relationships are about not letting an offense take hold in our heart. He said that if we discover, even while we are praying, that there is an offense between a brother and ourselves, we are to leave our gift at the altar and go do the work of forgiveness and reconciliation.[3] We are not to let the relationship just fall by the way. How many cut-offs in families or among friends would be prevented if we were open and honest and tenacious about addressing the problems between us?

A root of bitterness is so potent it will invade other people's gardens, and worst of all, it will choke the grace of God in my life. I will miss what I want most.

If cut-offs have been a pattern in your family or your present relationships, then you know the loneliness and lack of support that come from feeling chronically disconnected.

When I see the importance of forgiveness in the life of my own heart—or when I encounter the effect of neglecting to forgive—I am reminded of a rather haunting verse in the Book of Hebrews:

See to it that no one comes short of the grace of God; that no root of bitterness springing up causes trouble, and by it many be defiled.[4]

The heart is something of a garden that requires tending. Many things might have occasion to grow there. A root of bitterness is so potent it will invade other people's gardens, and worst of all, it will choke the grace of God in my life. I will miss what I want most.

But bitterness, I suspect, grows in the dark—a sneaky kind of thing that takes over before you know what's happening. So I often find myself praying, "Lord, show me . . . show me the hard places in my heart where I have become even a little bitter." When Stacy and I were first married, we were quick to ask each other's forgiveness. We kept very short accounts. And when we return to the humility of that now, in any form, I find the garden of our relationship flourishes again.

It's like someone has been pulling weeds.

THE PROBLEM OF FORGIVENESS

Forgiving the day-to-day slights and irritations that come your way is small potatoes compared to the work of forgiving serious injury from another person—of feeling betrayed by someone you love. The everyday stuff is what the Bible simply calls "bearing with" someone. But when the hurt has been costly and you may feel the impact for years to come—well, that is like getting a graduate degree in forgiveness.

The problem, so to speak, is that forgiveness offends our basic sense of justice. If we've been really hurt by someone we love, some voice in the core of our soul screams, "It's not fair. This is not right." And if we let the offender off the hook, then the record will never be set straight it seems. All hell will break loose again. We fear we will be stuck with at least one of two unpleasant possibilities.

"I'm left holding the bag." A woman whose husband had an affair explained to me that what galled her most was that he got the pleasure—and she got the pain. She felt she was left holding the bag. There is indeed a debt incurred with serious personal injury like this, and the question is a live one: What do we do about the wrong that's been done and the sense that someone should pay?

"I'll be victimized again." The strange thing about anger and unforgiveness is that they can become the only blanket that keeps us warm or that seems to cover the nakedness of our injuries. If we let that go, then what defense do we have? How will we ever venture out into life and feel protected from being hurt like that again? Many a crusty woman holds on to her anger because she's convinced it's all the armor she has.

What the Bible teaches about recompense can really come to our aid here. Recompense is an Old Testament word that acknowledges there is truly a debt to be paid. And amazingly enough, God promises to pay it. He says he will set the record straight. He speaks through the prophet Isaiah:

> Instead of your [former] shame you shall have a twofold recompense; instead of dishonor and reproach [your people] shall rejoice in their portion. Therefore in their land they shall possess double [what they had forfeited]; everlasting joy shall be theirs.
>
> For I the Lord love justice; I hate robbery and wrong with violence or a burnt offering. And I will faithfully give them their recompense in truth, and I will make an everlasting covenant or league with them. . . .
>
> Then I said, I have labored in vain, I have spent my strength for nothing and in empty futility; yet surely my right is with the Lord, and my recompense is with my God.[5]

The idea behind recompense is that God knows the injustice we feel. It offends him far more than it does us. And he is offering to repay the debt himself—in his way and his time. Perhaps you have heard that wonderful phrase often quoted from Joel: God will "restore to you the years that the . . . locusts have eaten."[6] So we don't have to just stand there holding the bag. We can genuinely bring the debt to him.

I remember a story told by an older missionary who had spent most of his life in Asia. He was bent out of shape over a man who kept neglecting to repay a significant sum of money he had borrowed. It became a chronic irritation. Finally, he prayed and told God he would release the debt to him. "Would you repay me the money that is owed here?" he asked the Lord. Over the next few years, God returned the exact amount. It was so clearly something God did that when the offender finally offered to pay back the money, the missionary could truthfully say, "You know, that debt has already been paid." He did not feel he could collect on the debt twice.

The one thing that is specifically forbidden is vengeance, the very human longing to get back at someone. Perhaps you know the expression, "I want him to pay for what he did." How much passion there can be in those words! But getting even, paying back—vengeance—is territory that God expressly reserves for himself. "Vengeance is Mine, I will repay," he says.[7] To try to get even is a dangerous business. We are playing God—stepping into a place that he claims as his alone.

GETTING REAL ABOUT FORGIVENESS

Maybe the reason that real forgiveness is a challenge is that the process is not all that neat and tidy. Or as they say, forgiveness is both an event and a process—a big "YES, I choose to forgive," followed by many little yeses as the months and years roll by.

I remember being surprised to read C. S. Lewis's admission that only on his deathbed did he finally feel free of the last vestige of anger toward his personal tutor in preparatory school, who had shamed him unmercifully. He had forgiven him earlier in his life, but the process of choosing to forgive again and again as different memories returned lasted throughout his life. Or as Sandra Wilson explains well, "I have discovered that forgiving can be a lot like packaging an octopus. Just about the time you think you have it all wrapped up, something else pops out!"[8]

Some injuries of the spirit have both a past and an ongoing present—and so forgiveness by necessity is a work in progress. A woman whose husband has been addicted to pornography forgives—but she may well be faced with the problem again. When she climbs into bed with her husband, you can be sure that she is making an ongoing choice to forgive and to rebuild trust. I often see women who have painful, even abusive events in their childhood that are hard to forgive—and they daily try to love and care for some of the same people who are still, shall we say, less than pleasant to be around. The big YES followed by many little yeses.

There is no small amount of confusion about what forgiveness actually is. The best description I've found of what we are saying when we choose to forgive a deep wound goes something like this:

> I am no longer looking to the one who hurt me to make it up to me. I am not waiting for this person to change or apologize. I release them from having to make me OK. I make the decision to look to God to make things right in my life. The person who hurt me is no longer God in my life.[9]

However we slice this pie, forgiving well means moving through the hurt and the legitimate anger that tells us we've been hurt, to a choice to release the person who inflicted the injury. Notice that I didn't say excuse. There's no effort to gloss over something here. Forgiveness is about looking the pain straight in the eye and saying, "God is bigger than this."

I find, personally, that there is nothing quite so helpful as a blank legal pad and a couple of hours. It's so helpful that about twice a year I take out my yellow pad and start to write, even when I can't think of anyone to forgive! I ask God to show me if there is anything I am holding against anyone, and I let my pencil do the talking. When he brings something to mind, I write about the pain I feel. I write about my choice to let this go, to let God carry this for me. Then I tear up the paper into a dozen little yellow pieces and go about my day. It's like taking a cool shower after jogging on a hot day.

Creating something concrete that symbolizes the letting go of an offense can be a tangible way of putting something difficult behind you. Occasionally, I encourage a woman to speak with someone they have struggled to forgive as a way of letting go and moving on. It could be called an I-have-come-to-realize conversation. There is no effort to blame—in fact, the emotional work of forgiving needs to be done ahead of time. But to share where you've come to with the person who seemed to stand in the way is a powerful experience, to say the least. So, for instance, the daughter of the demanding father might say, "I realize that I have worked all my life to measure up to a very high standard and I never felt I could. I can see that I need to let that go." Such words require nothing from the other person. All the pronouns are personal ones. Simply speaking I-have-come-to-realize words is an act of release and letting go— and a giant validation of moving forward.

Sometimes a person asks, "How can I tell when I've really forgiven?" Certainly, there is a new willingness to stop replaying the mental tapes of "how I was wronged." As they say, resentment actually means re-sentiment, meaning to rehearse the feeling over and over. In other words, I may have been a victim once, but the next forty-nine times I replay the home video in my mind are injuries by my own hands. I have a friend who claims he knows he has really forgiven when he can't remember the details anymore.

Lewis Smedes, in his book *Forgive and Forget,* gets right to the heart of the issue when he says, "You will know that forgiveness has begun when you recall those who hurt you and feel the power to wish them well."[10] When I can wish the best for them, I know I have traveled down the path of real forgiveness.

It seems like an impossible task when God tells us to love our enemies and bless those who harm us. Of all things, love an enemy! But blessing someone who has hurt us is actually our saving grace. If you've ever done that—asked God's blessing on someone who has hurt you—you know that even as you are speaking the words you feel the release in your soul. Talk about getting unstuck from something. To bless someone is to ask God to accomplish his purpose in their lives—with all the change and repentance and growth that entails. Only God is the one doing the work. You are free.

Have you thought that your willingness to forgive is really your affirmation of the power of God to do you good?

Have you thought that your willingness to forgive is really your affirmation of the power of God to do you good? What you are saying, in so many words, is that you realize God is able to do an end run around this injury, this betrayal, this pain, and bless your life. Anyway.

I should add that forgiveness is not a magic wand. Sometimes I hear a person say, "Well, it's true he had an affair, but he's really sorry. And his wife should forgive him." As though forgiveness would make all things new.

Even when she does forgive him, it takes time and distance to rebuild what is shattered in the betrayal of trust. You can see this clearly in the story of Joseph in the Book of Genesis. Sold by his brothers into slavery, Joseph had many years in prison to work through forgiving his brothers. And it's clear he did—he provided for them handsomely when they came to Egypt. But Joseph did not bare his soul to them. He did not weep on their shoulders when he felt tears sting his eyes. He waited to see what kind of change of heart God had worked in them.

The point, really, is that there is much more involved in reconciliation than in forgiveness. The two are not the same. Reconciliation requires two people who are willing to take ownership, in some way, for the problem. It means addressing the actual issues that led to the need to forgive in the first place. In being willing to forgive, we open our hearts to the possibility of a new relationship. We welcome change. But the only part that is under our control is the ability to forgive. As the Bible says, "So far as it depends on you, be at peace with all men" (emphasis mine).[11]

THE POTENTIAL IN FORGIVENESS

Anne Lamott admitted in an interview that forgiveness was not something she was "heavily into" when she first came to faith. There were a couple of people she refused to forgive. But God kept bringing up the issue, so to speak. In fact, he even arranged a few meetings and phone calls with people whom Anne had taken pains to avoid. It was like God set her up. He is "a tricky dance partner," she says.[12] Learning to forgive has played such a big role in her life that Anne likens forgiveness to meat tenderizer that has softened the fibers of her soul.

Forgiving well can actually bless the socks off you—in some surprising ways. I think, sometimes, there must be a blinding quality to harboring anger and unforgiveness, because when they are not blocking the view, the picture looks a bit different. The offending person comes into focus, almost for the first time—with his own batch of insecurities, foibles, and plain old sin.

Maybe your angry father didn't think you were a giant failure as a daughter. It could be that three martinis before dinner every night led to some terribly irresponsible words . . . and in fact, he saw himself as the woefully inadequate one.

Perhaps your older sister doesn't give you incessant advice about how to raise your children because you aren't much of a mother. The truth could be that she never felt she could do anything in life as good as you've done it—and here is one place where she knows a little more because she has lived longer.

When your husband had an affair last year, he really may not have been saying there is something deeply flawed in you. He honestly may have been grasping at anything that would make him feel like the man he used to be—though he sure picked a painful route.

Maybe your stepfather rides your case—even though he should know that as a college student you are old enough to make your own decisions. But he was on his own by the age of fifteen and he would have given anything to have someone care enough to give him some instructions. He doesn't know when to stop because he had no model for parenting himself.

Every one of these examples comes out of the life of a real woman. I do not offer the other person's perspective as a way of making excuses. In every situation here, there is something major to forgive. But forgiveness often allows a whole new interpretation to emerge.

In the process of forgiving, tiny little drops of understanding and even compassion come your way. Take them. They are God's way of letting you off the hook. Some of the conclusions we come to in the pain of being wronged are simply not accurate. Perhaps in seeing the other person's sin and weakness clearly, with some measure of empathy, God is whispering in your ear: *You really are not the unwanted . . . unloved . . . unvalued woman you thought you were.*

In speaking about forgiveness, I have written almost totally about offering forgiveness. There is another side to the coin, equally important—that of asking forgiveness. It is nearly guaranteed that any place in our lives where there is significant pain—we have been wronged by another—there is a commensurate amount of sin on our part. In other words, the pain rarely stops with us. We tend to pass it on. The most convincing argument for the fallenness of the human race is to see how automatic is our tendency to wound others from the pain of our own wounds. Sometimes, it is in the act of forgiving that the courage comes to look at our own sin honestly.

I once knew a woman who struggled for years under the weight of depression, always feeling she could never measure up. Not a good enough Christian. Not a good enough wife and mother. Her father's voice, "Do more . . . Do better," rang in her ears, and she almost hated him for it. As she began to acknowledge that and to forgive and let go, she heard the negativity in her own voice with her daughters. To ask their forgiveness was a major turning point in their relationship. "I realize," she said, "that I have set some impossible expectations for you to live up to, and I know how that feels. I want to say I am sorry. And I want to ask your forgiveness."

We are such broken people—all of us, both victim and agent—standing in need of the grace of God.

Have you noticed the way apologizing for your part in something softens your heart? Confession is good for the soul, as the saying goes. I think of owning my part as reaching into the center of the table and picking up a tangible piece of something I sense is mine—my negative attitude, my self-centered motivation, my fear. It's not *all* mine, but I do have to own my part. When I speak that, I can feel something release inside. I can tell my heart is softening. And occasionally, I think I hear a few angels cheer.

> He who conceals his sins does not prosper,
> but whoever confesses and renounces them finds mercy.[13]

Only Christians have the privilege of knowing they are blameless before God. They will never face the day when his finger is pointed at them in judgment. Ironically, though, Christians often find it hardest to admit when they are at fault in real life. We think we have to be perfect—or at least appear that way. As long as we are human and in conflict with another person, there will always be something worthy of a true apology and real change on our part. We may be blameless before God, but we can never be sinless—and that is a crucial distinction.[14] The reality of being forgiven means that we, of all people, have the freedom to admit where we are wrong.

In terms of all the heart softening that comes from admitting our own failures, let me underscore the magical quality of the words, "Will you forgive me?" Sometimes it's not enough to say, "I'm sorry." The words "Will you forgive me?" are needed to unlock the grudge. They are the conversational equivalent of a tennis match—they clearly put the ball in the other person's court. For one crucial moment, he has to look into his own heart and consider: Will I or won't I forgive? And when he says, "Yes, I forgive you," he is back in the game in a different way. He has let go of his resentment.

Truly forgiving, and being forgiven, is like pumice to the soul. As much strength as it takes to forgive and to seek someone's forgiveness, nothing keeps the heart in a softer, more pliable state. I want to be like the woman in Marnie's dream—warm and alive, with the wisdom that comes from the grace of forgiving well.

Listen with Your Heart

1. Take a few minutes and write about your most meaningful experience of being forgiven. What were the circumstances? How did you feel? What did you carry away with you?

2. Flip to the other side. Write the generalities of the experience you find hardest to forgive. Putting those two memories together, what about being forgiven helps you to forgive?

3. Many people live with a string of broken relationships, "cut-offs" they have permitted or felt powerless to prevent. Can you name any cut-offs in your extended family? What relationships do you have currently that are in need of repair or even estranged? What do broken relationships—past or present—cost you?

4. Read Matthew 5:21–24. To what relational principles is Jesus calling our attention?

5. How would you complete this sentence: "I want to forgive, but the fear that holds me back is . . ."?

6. Think of a difficult experience or relationship where God enabled you to forgive. How did that happen? What was the impact on your own heart and your relationship with God?

7. Colossians 3:12–15 is a compact picture of healthy relationships. What are you called to offer others?

8. From what does that stem in your own experience? (verses 12 and 13)

9. Being able to forgive has the potential to change the way you see yourself and/or the other person. Write about one set of perceptions you've seen altered by forgiveness.

9

SEXUALITY:
The Heart's Unsuspecting Mirror

May he kiss me with the kisses of his mouth!
For your love is better than wine. . . .
Draw me after you and let us run together!
The king has brought me into his chambers.

SONG OF SOLOMON 1:2–4

Take me to You, imprison me, for I
Except You enthrall me, never shall be free
Nor chaste except You ravish me.

JOHN DONNE

One of my more nervy friends frequently speaks to women on a matter of the heart that is rarely addressed in large groups. She speaks on sex. To women who have never enjoyed sex, she encourages them to "go for it." Sexual pleasure in the context of marriage is God's invention—his idea—and they are missing something wonderful in life if they settle for sex as an obligatory duty. She challenges them to consider that their attitudes toward sexual passion say something important about the state of their hearts. And then, finally, she says, "Picture an intimate moment with your husband.

Do you realize that the angels in heaven applaud this moment as something beautiful—a priceless work of art, a picture of the love and union that will one day be enjoyed between God and us?"

Women literally stand up and cheer when she is finished speaking.

I was curious at this response, so I asked her why she thought women actually cheered at the end of this unusual message. "I think it says how deeply women long to experience sexual pleasure without shame," she said. "Women long for the blessing of God in this area of their lives."

Indeed. There is something about sex, wouldn't you say, that just refuses to be separated from the rest of our lives. It spills over—it mirrors something beyond the moment. It touches the core. Not that sex is so utterly and terribly important, but our sexuality reflects our identity as God has made us male and female and in this way, touches so much that is not overtly sexual. At a profound level, sex is a window into the heart. Sex gives us a gauge for things that seem a world away from the experience—things like our ability to trust, our longing to be known, and the extent to which we have actually forgiven ourselves or someone else. There is something about passion, however it is expressed in life, that requires an open, inviting, set-free heart.

Certainly, we have all suffered from the futile attempt of the last thirty years to make sex a stand-alone commodity—as though it could be gored of its emotional and spiritual aspects. Sex can be treated as something that is about as personal as two airplanes refueling—just another way to connect for the moment. But our humanity shows up, and the emptiness speaks of something wrong, something missing. As one woman said of her promiscuous twenties, "I wish I hadn't given so much of myself. I feel that some of my experiences thinned my soul, and such an effect takes time to undo."[1] No matter how much our culture tries to pretend, we cannot keep ourselves from realizing that sex has both context and meaning—that in a sexual encounter, we are standing at the edge of something holy.

SEX AND THE LIFE OF THE HEART

The Bible makes a clear distinction between sensuality and being sensuous. Sensuality, which means an unrestrained sexual lust, is cautioned against. But to be a sensuous woman is a positive term. It means "to be alive to the pleasure received through the senses."[2] My nervy friend is right to encourage us to enjoy the blessing of God in our sexual lives. Sex is, indeed, a kind of window into the heart, albeit an unconventional one.

What does this mean for single women? How does a woman make a choice for celibacy, say, without shutting off her feeling of being female? Single women tell me that this is one of the hardest issues to sort through.

"I used to think that being single and not having sex with a man meant that I just neutered that part of my heart," one woman in her thirties explained. Then she realized how wrong that was and that the place it led her to didn't resemble life. "I've learned not to deny my sexual desires, but to walk with them through life as much as I can—meaning that I let myself enjoy the affirmation of a man, or rest in the strength he brings to the picture. Or talk with other women about sexual struggles. I can't divorce my sexuality just because I'm not having sex."

When it comes to a couple's sexual life, it's important to make a disclaimer: Not every sexual impasse reflects an issue of the heart. Not every woman who feels she would enjoy sex about twice a year has some emotional problem that keeps her willingly celibate. Sometimes there are genuine physiological differences in couples that greatly influence their desire for sex—a kind of cocktail of neurochemicals and hormones that vary widely from individual to individual. Physiology plays a huge role in the world of sexual passion.

For the first eighteen to thirty-six months of a marriage, we get the benefit of elevated levels of this romance cocktail. That seems just long enough to really bond as a couple. And since none of us could actually live in that rapture indefinitely, those levels settle into something more manageable, and we can make it to work on time again.

So couples may eventually discover that they have natural inclinations and a desire for sexual intimacy that vary considerably—and those differences can be physiologically based. A woman with a low sexual drive, for instance, is not defective in some way. But like any set of physical differences, it takes some work and consideration to accommodate both partners.

How much of a connection is there for you between your spiritual life and your sexual life—or do those seem like opposite ends of the planet?

Having said that, though, sex can provide a world of insight into our emotional lives and inner worlds. We act out the closeness we don't feel sometimes by quietly keeping our distance, hugging the side of the bed. Last week's argument never got resolved. The distance builds and the tension mounts. And while we may manage the kids' carpool and the family checking accounts and a host of other things, our sexual lives slide to the periphery and we hope our husbands won't mind all that much.

Have you been there? Who hasn't, at one time or another?

When you think about how you actually feel about sexual intimacy, what comes to mind? How much of a connection is there for you between your spiritual life and your sexual life—or do those seem like opposite ends of the planet? How much do you and your husband talk about the emotional impact of sex on him—on you?

Sometimes when I read the biblical words given to married couples about sex, I am amazed at how much of a given God meant for sex to be in our lives. Not an addendum, a luxury item, an afterthought, but a given. Something offered freely—like grace itself.

> The wife does not have authority over her own body, but the husband does; and likewise also the husband does not have authority over his own body, but the wife does. *Stop depriving one another,* except by agreement for a time that you may devote yourselves to prayer. (emphasis mine)[3]

In other words, you may have some profound disagreements between you. You may go without a lot of creature comforts. Many of your dreams may crash and burn. But through it all, keep coming together in this comforting, healing, physical way, God says. There is more happening in sex than you realize. This should be one safe harbor you can count on. This is one area of your life together where you must not withhold.

It's not unusual for a couple looking for some help with their relationship to come into therapy and say, "We don't communicate well." They try to talk—and it winds up in an argument. One person will complain that the other doesn't listen. Things get misinterpreted. Verbal communication breaks down. Often I will ask, "So how does all this affect your sexual intimacy?" And usually, two people stare back at me as if I have cotton in my ears. "What sexual intimacy?" they say.

It really is important to be able to talk together—to resolve conflicts and to understand each other's points of view. I would never discount the value of that kind of connection. But I am also a realist. And I wonder, could it be that sex is a language God gives that does not require words, so that even when we can't get our minds to meet, we are not left totally high and dry? I often think there is more than a little biblical wisdom in the lyrics of that country-and-western song, "Can't We Talk It over in Bed?" In many situations, we communicate through physical intimacy things we may forever lack the words to say.

The sexual relationship is, indeed, something offered freely, and perhaps that is why it can give us insight into our hearts. In the design of God, maybe it is all part of a package—so that if I pay attention to what's happening in my sexual life, I will also be drawn to deal with my real heart issues. And as God brings more freedom and cleansing to my heart, the most intimate relationship of my life will feel the effect.

There are so many ways in which issues of the heart can infect our sexual lives. Many things—from the past and the present—can play into the way we approach sexual intimacy.

When Sally met Mike, she was just coming off the breakup of a relationship with a man she felt sure she would marry. But what do you do when you discover the man you love is in love with another woman? You gather up what remains of your dignity and pride and you move on, right? Mike seemed to be everything the other guy was not. But Sally knew she wasn't wildly in love with Mike. They had many of the same interests; she admired him in important ways. But she didn't feel the same attraction. She had no inclination to do cartwheels when he walked into the room.

They had been married for five years now and by most counts, successfully so. Their only real arguments were about sex—and it was the same one, over and over. It wasn't just Sally's lack of desire. Mike understood that women could be different in that arena.

Something else was missing. Mike was beginning to wonder if he'd ever had Sally's heart.

Sexual intimacy tends to bring to the surface what is really happening—or not happening—in our hearts. Sex is a difficult place to hide. Sally discovered, as do many women, that she was not yet free to really give her heart to the man she married in the way she wanted. For any number of reasons, these women have shut down on the inside, and that emotional freeze shows up in their sexual lives.

A big emotional inhibitor for many women centers on the promiscuity of their pasts—even when sex was with the man who later became their husband. The problem is that sex was exciting, forbidden fruit back then. Once married, sex became just part of the warp and woof of everyday life, and women often complain they cannot resurrect the same interest. Memories of pleasurable sex got set in the wrong context, it seems. It's like the whole sexual experience got sprinkled with the dust of guilt and shame.

> *Physical intimacy cannot be a prize to be earned when one is thin enough or smart enough or good enough. It is meant to be a given.*

"I am just beginning to realize," one wife said, "that what I had to give was good. My sexuality was good. It was blessed by God. But I let myself be used sexually many times before I married. I feel that I prostituted myself to keep the relationships I had with men." She carried that exact mind-set into marriage with her. On her honeymoon, she said, she "could hear the jail bars coming down." She saw herself facing a lifetime of feeling used.

So it is that the issues of our sexuality bleed over into matters of the heart. One cannot be unraveled without addressing the other. Big questions arise. Do you see yourself as a woman who deserves to be loved and cherished? Have you let yourself receive the forgiveness of God where you most need to? Is your sexuality a gift of God that you honestly feel is a good gift?

Another issue of the heart that sex surfaces is both the longing to be known and, ironically, the fear of being known. For a woman who feels she must be something special to be loved—that no one could really love her as she is without the adornments of her achievements or the image she has worked hard to cultivate—sex feels like a loss of control, a nakedness that will surely lead to rejection. The need of the heart becomes one of learning to trust God and trust this man who has been brought into her life. Physical intimacy cannot be a prize to be earned when one is thin enough or smart enough or good enough. It is meant to be a given.

When a woman has had a really negative sexual experience, she often carries powerful fears of being used and abandoned. Perhaps you remember the words from a song in the musical version of *Les Misérables,* sung by a young single mother who works in a factory to support her daughter. In her song, Fantaine remembers the man she loved one summer, who became the father of her child. Their time together was like a dream, and the pain of being loved and left is expressed in one line from the song that brings tears to the eyes of everyone who hears it:

> But he was gone when autumn came.[4]

These are the kind of fears of abandonment that get dragged into the bedroom. Being loved and left leaves a powerful impression on the heart. Sex feels like a set-up to be hurt again—and unconsciously, you expect one thing to follow the other.

Marie came to see me claiming that she was bored with sex and because of that she and her husband fought all the time. When she talked about her life, it was the story of a trail of men who had used her sexually, beginning with an uncle in her childhood. Her boredom with sex was really a mask for the fear she felt that she couldn't trust her husband. Maybe he, too, would up and leave.

"Can you picture what it would have felt like to be so cherished by a man that he wanted to protect your innocence?" I asked her.

A little trail of tears trickled down her cheeks at the thought of what that would have been like. She realized that she was meant to be able to trust a man, to feel that he had her interests at heart. I asked her what she saw in her husband that was trustworthy, and actually, there were many things.

"Suppose you have an honest conversation with him about your past and your fears of being abandoned," I suggested, "and give him the chance to offer you what you've had so little of—the protection and reassurance of a man who is genuinely different from those you have known." Marie was surprised to see that her feelings about sex actually changed when there was more honesty and understanding between the two of them—when she could talk about the heart issues that for her were profoundly connected with sex.

What we are sometimes slow to realize is that while sexual intimacy may bring to light the fractures of our spirits, God has also designed sex with its own healing property. One lovely, tender verse in the Old Testament gives us a very human glimpse into this reality. Isaac, the son of Abraham, has been given a wife not long after the death of his mother, Sarah. The story of how Isaac was brought together with Rebekah is wonderful in itself. And it ends with this verse:

> Then Isaac brought her into his mother Sarah's tent, and he took Rebekah, and she became his wife; and he loved her; *thus Isaac was comforted after his mother's death.* (emphasis mine)[5]

It is a witness to the goodness of God that he would provide a salve for the wounds of the heart in the very nature of experiencing the love—the physical love—of a good man in your life.

MEN AND SEX

I often wish that I could videotape the conversations I am afforded with men through the rare privilege of hearing them talk frankly about their lives—their sexual lives. I catch myself, sometimes, on the verge of saying, "Really? Is that the way a man feels about sex?" I realize, as I listen, how sex adds up emotionally for a man. I wish I could have understood more much earlier in my life.

The best way I have to explain what I hear is that a man's psyche is a seamless fabric. A woman learns early on to divide her life into parts, so that if she feels like a sexual failure, well, at least she's doing fairly well as a mother or a friend or a graduate student or a Bible study leader. She'll try to pick up the sexual piece later. But men tend to see themselves as a whole entity. If they feel sexually inadequate, then that inadequacy seeps into every other corner of their experience. If their sexual lives are floundering, then, they reason, the rest cannot be too far behind.

So, for example, a woman might say she is happy in her marriage and yeah, sure, sex is not all that great and hasn't been in a long time. Her husband would tend to say their marriage is in jeopardy. There is much more resting on the sexual connection— for most men, anyway—because sex says more to a man about himself.

George Gilder, in his book *Men and Marriage,* helped me understand why more is riding on sex for men than for women. He explains that women take their bodies and their sexuality far more for granted than men do. Women's bodies are more versatile. We can give birth and breast-feed our children, whereas men have only one sexual act—intercourse. A woman can relate to a man sexually whether she is into the experience or not. If a man cannot perform sexually, it's a "show-stopper," as they say. Gilder writes,

Men must perform . . . the man is less secure sexually than the woman because his sexuality is dependent on action, and he can act sexually only through a precarious process difficult to control. For men the desire for sex is not simply a quest for pleasure. It is an indispensable test of identity.[6]

That theme is repeated over and over when men talk frankly about sex. If sex is a problem in a man's marriage, it's not just a problem in his marriage. It means he must not be much of a man.

A man can be the soul of objectivity in most every arena of his life—except sex. He can explain the irritable words his wife spoke at dinner as the aftermath of her hard day. It's not about him. When she overspent on her credit card, he does not necessarily hear a personal message in that mistake. But there is something deeply personal about being turned down in his overture for sexual intimacy. It feels as though he, himself, his very person is being rejected. And only after he works and works to get past that awful feeling does he stand a chance of hearing that his wife does actually, in fact, have a splitting headache. This is, at least, how many men feel.

> If sex is a problem in a man's marriage, it's not just a problem in his marriage. It means he must not be much of a man.

From a man's standpoint, the absence of a warm sexual connection with his wife, one he can confidently count on, injects the most toxic of emotions into their relationship. His wife does not see it that way. Sex is just less important to her or she has a lot on her mind these days—that kind of thing. A man experiences this very differently. If his sexual need goes perennially begging, he feels as though his wife is *withholding,* just as surely as if he came to the table every night hungry and she served him an empty plate. The misery is about the same. You can understand why anger and resentment begin to fester in big ways.

Perhaps it would help to "listen in" on some of the comments that men make about how the lack of a good sexual life feels to them:

I work for days to build a connection with my wife. We talk. I catch up on what's happening in her life. We are starting to feel close. I start to think, Tonight's the night! I look forward to sexual intimacy. Then it gets ruined by what seems like the simplest thing—a headache, a little spat. We start the process over again. Sex feels like a merit badge I have to earn.

My wife talks sometimes about the ways that I have hurt her—and I know I have. But our sexual life is a perennial pain to me, and somehow that doesn't count because it is pain she can't see.

Sometimes I get angry with God because he has given me this sexual need but he has limited me to one woman on the planet—and it's rarely very good with her. Yet I'm not supposed to look elsewhere.

I share these comments, not as a guilt trip, but to validate the experience of men. Sex is a window into a man's heart, too, but what you see when you look in is genuinely different. I am convinced that if we could hear a man's heart—if we could feel his sexual vulnerability—it would melt our defenses in all the right ways. It would touch our empathy. And sexual intimacy would probably assume a larger place in our lives.

THE SOUL OF SEX

It amazes me, sometimes, that God could have chosen sexual intimacy as the small drama that most closely reflects the large drama of his relationship with us. But he has. Sex is a living object lesson that reminds me on some regular basis that God seeks union with me. I await the Bridegroom, and one day we will dance at the marriage feast of the Lamb together. Such is the biblical imagery that foreshadows a much bigger mystery, enacted in small, intimate ways in the passion between a man and a woman.

The right word really is *mystery*—a word that, in the biblical sense, does not mean "baffling" or "shrouded from our view." Rather a mystery, as God uses the word, means something revealed expressly for our understanding. A mystery is not about God concealing something, but rather revealing it and drawing us to himself through the mystery. So, for instance, the reality of Christ actually living in us is a mystery.[7] That regular Gentiles can be included in the family of God, through Christ—this is a mystery.[8] And yet one more, this time pictured in the relationship between a man and a woman:

> For this cause a man shall leave his father and mother, and shall cleave to his wife; and the two shall become one flesh. This mystery is great; but I am speaking with reference to Christ and the church.[9]

Physical intimacy, set in its true context, takes us straight to the heart of God, because the necessary components of trust and faithfulness and passion belong, first and foremost, to him. Sex is a drama that mirrors the sacrificial love of God—a spiritual reality so beautiful, so profound, it will take the whole of our lives to comprehend.

Have you thought, for instance, about the uncanny parallel between sex and prayer? We rarely utter both words—sex and prayer—in the same sentence, as though the first had to do with church and worship and holiness and the second . . . well, that's another story. And yet, in your prayer life, are there not elements of passion and surrender, the laying bare of the soul before the Lord, with whom you have an exclusive relationship, unlike any other? The parallel is just too clear: Worship and sex are two bookends of human experience, both meant to draw us to the Lord and to each other. So the sixteenth-century poet John Donne could rightly end his sonnet with words that sound like those spoken to a lover—except they are spoken to the Lord:

Take me to You, imprison me, for I
Except You enthrall me, never shall be free
Nor chaste except You ravish me.[10]

Sometimes I remind myself that God chose to reveal himself as a Hebrew, not as a Greek. Hebrews *experienced* truth—mind, soul, and body—they did not reduce it to a mental exercise, as did the Greeks who so influenced our culture. There is no split between body and soul in Christianity. Unlike the Romans, Christians buried their dead out of respect for the body. Missionaries built hospitals to care for the sick, because the body is not unimportant or evil or immaterial. The body is made to glorify the Lord, as well as the soul, the apostle Paul said.[11] Christianity has always had a valid and special place for the body.

That is why sex has a truly sacramental aspect to it—a reality that our grandparents understood better than we. The old wedding vows always included this telling phrase spoken between a man and a woman: "With my body I thee worship." There is one whole book of the Bible devoted to the pleasures of sexual intimacy, in terms that make most of us blush.

So God gives sexual intimacy as a kind of physical patterning— an acting out of a spiritual mystery that hints of the utter pleasure we will know one day in the presence of the Lord. For now, we have an experience that bonds us for life—body and soul—with the heart of another human being.

We have a frame that holds us together when the days grow dark and there are no words strong enough to make everything all right. We have a place of shelter, healing, passion, and dare I say it, grace.

Listen with Your Heart

1. How do you see your sexuality as a window into your heart? In what way is that thought freeing, or encouraging, or threatening, or challenging?

2. What do you think happens in the heart of a woman whose sexuality is given too freely, in an illicit way? What effect does that have on her?

3. Read Song of Solomon 1:2–4. What desire do you see mirrored here?

4. In Song of Solomon 7:1–10, the husband shares his enjoyment of his wife. How does this passage make you feel? What kind of freedom do you observe here?

5. When have you experienced sex as healing in some way? What was being communicated to you in a physical way?

6. Ask your husband to share with you what sexual intimacy communicates to him. What messages does he hear? How did you feel about what he said?

7. How does the reality that sexual intimacy mirrors our intimacy with God, our longing to reunite with him, affect the way you feel about sex?

THE WISE HEART

10

LOVING BEYOND REASON

Love anything, and your heart will certainly be wrung and possibly be broken. If you want to make sure of keeping it intact, you must give your heart to no one. It will not be broken; it will become unbreakable, impenetrable, irredeemable. . . . The only place outside Heaven where you can be perfectly safe from all the dangers and perturbations of love is Hell.

C. S. LEWIS

We don't mend each other's brokenness; we just hold it tightly.

M. CRAIG BARNES

The real gymnasium of the heart is our closest relationships. Our hearts are safe until love enters the picture. It takes the thought of a close relationship to stir our longings. To ignite our fears. To place our hearts at risk. The hope in becoming a strong woman with a soft heart is that God would set us free to love—lavishly and with wild abandon—the people he puts into our lives. That's what we've been made for. But loving well is no small assignment.

In the movie *Anna and the King*, there is the undercurrent of a love story so beautiful—and so tragic—it has few parallels in recent films. Perhaps you remember how the story goes. A young village girl has been chosen to be one of the king of Siam's wives, the newest member of his harem. Only she is deeply in love with a man from her small town. They have plans to marry. But any woman chosen by the king has no other choice. She is led in great pomp and procession, tears streaming down her face, to the king's palace to become his newest wife.

Her heart, however, remains with the man she had hoped to marry. They meet clandestinely—a dangerous act of treason. Anna, who knows the king well, cautions the girl not to do this risky thing. It could cost her life. In one poignant response she explains why the risk to love is one she must take. She says,

If love were a choice, who would ever choose such exquisite pain?

This story often comes to mind, especially when I confront the courage love requires. Love is such exquisite pain. It does not come cheaply—not the real kind, anyway. Love anything, C. S. Lewis said, and your heart will surely be wrung.

Love is costly—especially in marriage, the closest of relationships. The blending of two lives changes the whole landscape. Other cherished loyalties play second fiddle. Lifelong dreams may be seriously amended. Death or divorce will feel like someone ripped your skin off. Loving someone is the one venture in life in which the more you succeed, the more you have to lose. It is so tempting to keep your heart in reserve. To hedge your bets seems a reasonable choice in the face of things. But then, whoever said love was reasonable?

I learned a lot about love from my friend Pam, whose husband was diagnosed with a brain tumor, as I mentioned in an earlier chapter. In battling cancer, life gets compacted, crystallized—and sometimes you find that the disease brings things into sharper, clearer focus. Pam realized she had a clear choice to make. She could hold back and distance herself from Tim, and if he died, perhaps she would feel less pain. Or she could choose to love for all she was worth—and trust God with the outcome. She wrote,

When Tim first got sick and we realized how serious it was, I remember thinking, "This may be my one chance to love a man and to give myself to all marriage has to offer. I can either hold back and protect my heart from further pain down the road or I can go for broke and love like there is no tomorrow—because there may not be."

I decided I'd rather be heartbroken on the other side and have tasted all the possibilities—than held back, not risked and never known.

I'd rather be heartbroken . . . than to hold back and refuse to take the risk to love. Isn't that the choice each of us faces in our closest relationships—the temptation to keep our hearts on the shelf and maybe spare ourselves some pain? Since Tim's death, I find myself looking at people I love through different eyes. I realize a bit of what Pam saw: I don't have forever. I may not even have tomorrow. The choice to give myself to really loving someone is now—not later. Now is the time to do the work that real relationships take.

After Tim died, Pam said his absence on some days was so huge it felt like there was an elephant in the room. She was aware that the choice to squeeze all the joy that could be extracted out of the little time they had made his loss only more real. But she was not sorry she had gone for broke. "I think that love breeds life," she said, "and though Tim is gone, the love we shared so enriched my life. Without a doubt, it was worth it. I would do it all again."

THE MANDATE TO LOVE

The capacity to love—to really give ourselves to someone in a marriage, or even in a friendship—is what God made us for. He calls us, first of all, to risk our hearts with him. "God rescued us from dead-end alleys and dark dungeons. He's set us up in the kingdom of the Son he loves so much."[1] To breathe the air there is to be increasingly set free, but set free for a purpose—to love others out of the love we've been given. In letting ourselves be loved, we are able to love. As Romans says,

> We also exult in our tribulations, knowing that tribulation brings about perseverance; and perseverance, proven character; and proven character, hope; and *hope does not disappoint, because the love of God has been poured out within our hearts.* (emphasis mine)[2]

My point is that the good work of God in our hearts is to free us to love others without all the costly preoccupation of having to pose and posture and protect ourselves. God would make us extraordinary lovers. In fact, he gives the world the right to judge if we actually know him, not by what we know about him, but by our love for each other. What a sobering thought! "By this all men will know that you are My disciples, if you have love for one another," Jesus said.[3] The greatest evidence that we know God is relational—specifically, the power to love against all odds.

Loving and being loved is easy enough to begin, but much harder to sustain. When I studied the ins and outs of family therapy, I discovered a concept that explains the difficulty in relationships, and also argues, indirectly, for the existence of God. The idea is that love in a close relationship between two people is like a two-legged stool. It is inherently unstable. There is too much disappointment to sustain the weight. So our tendency is to form a triangle, by turning to a third party in some way. We often pull in a child or an in-law, and while that absorbs some of the pressure, it tends to cause more problems than it solves. Much of family therapy is about dissolving triangles and getting each party to relate directly to the other.

This observation on families fascinates me. I think it reveals something of the mind and heart of God—that he designed marriage, and really any close relationship, as a true threesome. It's meant to be a triangulated affair with him as the fulcrum of the triangle, the one who bears the real weight. That there is someone to turn to when you are disappointed in a relationship is not just pretty theology. It's the actual truth, the original design. As Solomon wrote in the Book of Ecclesiastes,

> Two are better than one. . . . For if either of them falls, the one will lift up his companion. . . . A cord of three strands is not quickly torn apart.[4]

In the truest sense, two people in a relationship are never enough. Love, on a human level, always proves incomplete. We need access to love greater than our own.

THE HIDDEN RISK IN LOVE

The risk in love is a bit like an old memory I have of my first real official date. A school dance was the occasion, one of those anxiety-ridden affairs that provides the first corsage to dry on your bedroom mirror. Somewhere in the middle of our enchanted evening, though, this young man decided that he was smitten with a lovely blonde whose eyes matched her blue suede dress. I went home with a friend. I have to add that I recovered quickly from the experience. I would not bore you with an old recollection except that, symbolically, the heart of our fear in love is much like this: We may be left, literally or figuratively, dancing alone. *This relationship, this friendship, this marriage is something I can do without. You, honey, I can do without.*

The risk of rejection pushes up the price of love. Marriage represents, perhaps, our greatest risk in loving another person well. In marriage, we bet the farm. In sickness and in health, for richer for poorer—such awesome vows in the face of the great unknown.

Maybe it really takes all those roses and a wedding cake to steel our courage to walk back down that aisle together and out into real life. For as much as we pledge on that lovely day—there will be times when we fail each other profoundly.

I see this, of course, in my own marriage. When Stacy and I were first married, one of our pet names for each other was "honey sinner," a term of endearment that helped in countless ways. We need the reminder that we are each married to a real live sinner. It polishes the shine off the picture in an appropriate way.

Marriage represents, perhaps, our greatest risk in loving another person well. In marriage, we bet the farm.

When I listen to a couple struggling in their relationship, I am often struck by the intricacy of the drama that develops between two people in this, the most delicate territory of their hearts. It's like flying alongside a man and woman who jumped out of a plane at the same moment and got the lines of their parachutes tangled on the way down. You hope they can sort this out before they hit the ground with a thud.

What often emerges in their struggle is an odd paradox. In the strangest sort of grace-filled way, their wounds match. Inevitably, one person's pain ignites the other person's greatest fear or deepest shame. The man who fears his wife's anger like the plague is married to a woman who struggles to keep emotional equilibrium. Or the woman whose father left the family when she was ten feels abandoned by her ambitious husband's love affair with his job. If someone could x-ray the hearts of two people at odds with each other, I suspect their wounds would coordinate like matching jogging outfits.

I think of one couple whose story is like many. When Denny was growing up, he managed to escape his parents' tragic life together by sheer gutsy determination and hard work. He pushed himself relentlessly. And while all that paid off in his work, it was killing his marriage. His wife was a quiet, sensitive, intelligent woman who felt she was no match for Denny's harsh words. Laura retreated and retreated and retreated—until Denny felt they were little more than roommates.

To disentangle the lines of their parachutes, Denny and Laura each had to walk into the territory of their deepest fears. That meant letting go of the old way they had always done life. Denny grew up like a little marine—strength was his savior. To be tender and compassionate with a woman felt like stepping into outer space—way out of control. And Laura had survived her childhood by hiding behind a good book and avoiding life. To believe that she actually had the strength to meet Denny toe-to-toe—and to appeal to his dormant tenderness—was a big step. But then, real love always is.

In the gracious design of God, a relationship becomes the crucible for our own personal transformation, which simply might not happen any other way. For what the other person most needs from us will require wrestling our own fear to the floor. To scratch their itch is, at first, to reopen our own wounds in life. It can feel like death. It can make us very dependent on God. The person we love can look, at times, like the enemy. In other words, your own risky growth not only blesses you—it eventually becomes the balm that most powerfully touches the wounded heart of the one you love. Such is the merciful wisdom of God in our lives.

> Marriage . . . is not a clever system of protection in which another person is interposed between ourselves and the pain of living. . . . The person may actually become the source or focus of more suffering than we ever bargained for, the very vessel from which our own humiliation is poured. It is true of all intimacy, but especially of marriage, that it creates the unique and miraculous circumstances in which suffering cannot be extricated from love.[5]

The suffering aspect of love applies more broadly than marriage—it is true of all intimacy. It's intrinsic to intimacy—part of the deal. I listened recently to two young professional women discuss why their friendship had been so complicated. Before they became good friends and roommates, they talked about how their racial differences might pose some problems. But neither was prepared for the subtle ways that living together exposed their own racism. Now they were running smack into the things that had irritated them the most—about white people, about black people. "We can't tell you how close we have come to walking out on this friendship," they admitted. Indeed, it is so easy to withdraw or give up when the going gets hard. But a commitment to love means hanging in there.

Love anything, C. S. Lewis said, and your heart will surely be wrung. You would think that such bending and stretching—such suffering—would do you in, like an ice pick that chipped away until nothing was left. But risky love works by an inverse principle. Our hearts become larger in the process. The more we love, the more we are able to love. We are not depleted, but strangely replenished. Set free. Given more. As the psalmist says, "I will run the way of thy commandments, when thou shalt enlarge my heart."[6]

THE PRACTICAL FACES OF LOVE

One thing I love about the Bible is the way it forces my hand in the important places of my life and insists I put shoe leather to what I know. Nowhere is this more true than in the world of relationships. Many people think that the disciple John had the closest relationship with Jesus of any of those who followed him. John wrote often about the love of God—he even identified himself by one simple telling phrase as "that disciple whom Jesus loved." And in his later life, John said that a person cannot even make the claim to love God and close his heart off to his brother. He can't say he loves God and refuse to love his brother.[7] Those two things won't mix.

So having a heart that is freed to love passionately, sacrificially, courageously, is pretty central. Let me offer a couple of practical aspects that tend to put flesh on the concept of loving well.

Love Has Space

The French priest who began the L'Arche communities, which minister to the severely handicapped, gives the best analogy I know of the importance of closeness and distance in a relationship. He says we must hold each other as we would hold a wounded bird. If we grip too tightly, we will crush the life out of the other person. And if we don't hold securely enough, of course, the relationship will falter altogether.[8]

In other words, love has space. In a close relationship, we have to recognize the part of the equation that uniquely belongs to the other person. It's their choice, their feelings, their responsibility, their painful past—that kind of thing. I find that especially hard to do sometimes. My tendency is to step in too quickly. To resist the urge to fix someone I love takes buckets of restraint, especially when an insight crosses my mind I think they just can't live without. But to fix them, to offer advice or help not asked for, is to invade their territory—to infringe on this invisible sort of space.

One careful distinction in a couple of Greek words from the Book of Galatians has been of enormous help. In one verse, Paul instructs us to bear each other's *burdens,* which means those heavy boulders of responsibility or pain that befall every person from time to time. We are to share the extra heavy trials of life. Right in the same chapter, however, Paul makes a curious statement: "Each man must bear his own load." That sounds contradictory until you realize that the word for *load* means "knapsack." Each of us has a knapsack to carry through life that is uniquely our own.

Have you ever thought of yourself as toting a knapsack through life? And the person you love, or a close friend, or someone you work with each day also has a knapsack that he or she alone can carry. In your knapsack are the responsibilities, the choices, the set of life circumstances, the feelings and opinions that belong to you. No one can forgive but you. No one can deal with the pain in your past but you. No one can really make you happy, or ruin your life. The choices that shape the way you see the picture are uniquely yours.

Invading the space of someone we love . . . shows a fundamental lack of respect. And disrespect eats away at the core of a relationship.

I remember working with a younger woman who had been married a few years—just long enough to discover that her husband did not have the consistency in his spiritual life she felt he should. She was intent on getting him to improve his devotional life. She felt their relationship suffered because of it. And she was determined that he take steps to bring this up to par.

I was getting a little confused. Was she satisfied with her own devotional life? Hers was fine, she assured me. "It's my husband's that's lacking," she emphasized again. "My *husband's* devotional life is the problem," she said, as if something were wrong with my hearing.

I took a deep breath and asked her if she brushed his teeth.

I think you get what I mean. Her husband's connection with God is a responsibility he carries in his knapsack. A choice he makes—as personal as the practice of brushing his teeth. And God won't let us dip into another person's knapsack.

Occasionally, I see a wife try to cajole her husband into regular exercise and losing weight. I watched a friend insist on monitoring another friend's use of time. I have known more than one man who would follow his wife around the house with a steady verbal pelting until she shared his precise opinion—or pretended she did. Invading the space of someone we love—dipping into his or her knapsack—shows a fundamental lack of respect. And disrespect eats away at the core of a relationship.

I find it personally helpful to recognize the places in a close relationship where I am powerless. I call those moments of insight "the blessed freedom of powerlessness." They are meant to be embraced. Realizing that I feel helpless is the cue that the choices involved legitimately belong to the other person, and I need to take a step back. To leave that space—to leave the ball in their court where it truly belongs—is an act of respect. It's like singing Aretha Franklin's old song: R-E-S-P-E-C-T. "I respect you enough to believe you have it in you to deal with that."

A little space can be the greatest compliment you pay someone.

Love Contains Both "Yes" And "No"

Strength and tenderness are two fascinating aspects in the dynamics of a relationship. To be a strong woman with a soft heart implies a mastery of both—an ease with being firm when we need to be, without losing the inner grace that really feels for the other person.

I often find that when a woman has been hurt in a close relationship she develops a hardness, an armorlike protective coating around her heart. She's scared to give a compliment or dish out words of praise. A warm bear hug would be letting down her guard. Enthusiastic sex might be read the wrong way, as though her pain didn't matter and she was ripe for being taken advantage of again in some way. So she backs up and keeps her emotional distance—offering only a kind of strength that says, "You will not hurt or disappoint me again." The other person, usually, feels as if he is standing outside a candy store with his nose pressed against the pane, starving for something he can't have.

Too much softness leans the other way. A woman who is all heart will give and give and give, and ask for too little in return. Strangely enough, when she says "No," she feels like the bad one, the wicked witch of the west. She is well-versed in the other person's pain—like empathy on steroids—but not so acquainted with her own. She is the proverbial woman who loves too much. Sometimes she merely moves through life with a lot of unmet needs. In the worst situations, though, a woman who has not discovered her rightful strength can be mightily manipulated by those whose radar easily detects the person who can't say "No."

What I'm really saying is that close relationships always contain generous measures of strength and softness, of yes and no. Love in a fallen world utterly requires them both.

Sometimes I think of this principle in the light of an old, very useful phrase coined by the philosopher Francis Schaeffer. Each of us, he said, is a "glorious ruin." Isn't that an incredibly accurate phrase? Don't the two words *glory* and *ruin* describe with painful accuracy what you live with every day in yourself and in those you love? For we do bear the glory of God imprinted on the image of our souls. To fall in love with someone is to be given a glimpse of the potential for the glory God put there originally. And yet we can't be with ourselves or someone we love for long without seeing another reality equally true: That image has been so marred in the fall and the stain of sin that sometimes, it's a crying shame.

That we are glorious ruins could just be the leftover notes of a theology class, or it can actually shape the intricacies of how we love each other in a decent way. In other words, if I really accept that this person I love will remain a glorious ruin until heaven restores the flawless beauty intended. Then, naturally, I will be saying both "Yes" and "No" in the relationship. We can't live together in a fallen world without addressing the things that seem to arise out of the ruin—not the glory. The strength to say "No" is required in order to love well. It's part of the equation. But we never give up our glimpse of the other person's glory. So we are always inviting, affirming, saying a big "Yes" to the best that God placed in them.

In a practical sense, then, a woman can refuse to tolerate her husband's angry outpouring—and she can also offer him the warmth of her bed, or the pleasure of her company. A friend can make it clear she wants to be loyal—but she doesn't want to be used in the process. A husband can hold his wife when she cries about something important to her—and he can still insist she stop charging up their credit cards.

In fact, real love requires the act of saying "No" at points. I once knew a woman who had struggled in her relationship with her mother for years. Her mother was the picture of the proper southern woman. Her words, though, were so critical and undermining that it took days after each visit for my friend to mend the lacerations of her mother's verbal jabs. But my friend was a Christian; her mother was not. And so she quietly endured, seeing her role as that of keeping the peace. She got to the point where she just could not face another round with her mother. To salvage the relationship and to keep her own soul intact, she had to speak up. Saying "No" to the verbal dumping was the first step in really loving her mother. A boundary like this has to be in place—otherwise, there is no space for two people to enjoy each other. Saying "No" actually allows you to say "Yes" in a bigger way.

Loving someone well is a kind of tending of the relationship, not unlike cultivating a garden. The relationship itself is almost a third being: not you, not the other person, but a living thing itself. For the sake of the relationship—for the sake of love itself—you offer the warmth and attention that would allow something good to grow, even though past hurt can make you wary. But the relationship, like any good garden, needs cultivation. And similarly, honesty insists that you tell the truth about the weeds taking over in certain spaces. Any real relationship will take some back-breaking work in the hot sun with a hoe in your hand. A good gardener knows that if she ignores the weeds, they take over. The reward comes in small moments of intimacy and connectedness—moments only, as elusive as any summer butterfly—but they do come. We just cultivate the garden as best we can. And try to be patient.

Exquisite pain that love is, it is forever interwoven with the risk of offering your heart to another person, who sometimes tramps all over it. Love anything . . . and your heart will be wrung. The more you succeed at love—the more you will have to lose. But honestly, would playing it safe and hedging your bets take you any place you really wanted to be? And as painful as love can be, could wisdom be won by any other means?

Listen with Your Heart

1. When are the times in a close relationship that you are most reminded of the exquisite pain loving someone well entails?

2. In your closest relationship, what would it look like to love more lavishly, with less self-protection?

3. Read 1 John 4:17–21, which is the apostle John's strongest treatise on loving others. What does he say would be missing from our lives if we understood God's love?

4. Try putting John's words in verse 20 in your own words. What did you feel as you wrote your own paraphrase?

5. In your closest relationship, how do your wounds in life ignite the wounds in the other person?

6. How would tackling your own fear bring some small measure of healing or grace in this other person? How do your wounds match?

7. If love has space, then do you need to give more space to someone you love, or do you need more space? In either case, what would that look like?

8. If your heart had actual walls around it, would those walls be too thick—meaning that it's hard to get close to you? Or would those walls be too thin—meaning that you are more easily taken advantage of and you require too little of others? How would you want it to be different?

11

LIVING BEYOND FEAR

Taking a new step, uttering a new word is what people fear most.

FYODOR DOSTOEVSKY

And the day came when the risk it took to remain tight in the bud was more painful than the risk it took to bloom.

ANAIS NIN

> The LORD is my light and my salvation;
> Whom shall I fear?
> The LORD is the defense of my life;
> Whom shall I dread?

PSALM 27:1

Sue hid in the shadows of the talent God gave her for most of her life—and for understandable reasons, really. The daughter of two parents who were born deaf, Sue became their ears. She also adopted her parents' code, the one most deaf people live by: Stay with what you know for certain. Don't reach too far. Something terrible may happen if you do. Sue's parents never changed jobs; they rarely even took a vacation. They passed on to their children the rules of life as they knew them. Venturing forth into the world beyond was, at best, riddled with anxiety.

In spite of this, Sue did things her parents could only dream of—like going to college, living in many places, leading professional workshops. But Sue was a bundle of fear. Every new or risky thing she did required her to do battle with the taboos of her childhood. Failure was simply proof she should never have tried in the first place.

Her frustration was evident the first time I talked with her. Here she was at thirty-eight with a master's degree she had never put to use, in a mindless job well beneath her abilities. "What have you always wanted to do?" I asked her, searching for the thing that would bring the spark back in her eyes.

"You won't believe this," she began, "but I have wanted for years to teach middle school." (She was right—I didn't believe her at first.) Then she went on to tell me all the reasons why that was too much to ask.

I watched Sue light up at the thought of teaching—she knew it was in her blood. And then I thought to myself: *Isn't this what we do so often?* Some little chorus of fears sets up shop in our brains, and like a broken record, the old voices whisper in our ears a hundred silly reasons why we—of all people—just cannot do that. *Other women maybe, but not us. Something terrible will happen.* Fear can bring such bondage to our lives.

To tell you the truth, I thought that feeling afraid was something I would outgrow—like a coat two sizes too small. And I have matured beyond some of my fears. But mostly, I have discovered what it is to experience the grace of God while actually doing the thing that makes me take a deep breath. I no longer see the smiles of confident women and think they must be made of sturdier stuff. I know, a little more anyway, that behind those smiles sits the same basic set of insecurities and self-doubt that I tote through life. And that really does help.

Some of the most profitable experiences of my life have centered around fear—walking through the messiness of it all and trusting God. Sometimes I find that the best thing that can happen to me is a sharp dose of the thing I have long avoided—and long feared. Like, for instance, the night I bombed a speaking engagement overseas.

For many people, I guess, speaking in public ranks right near the top of their worst fears. In self-defense, I tend to overprepare when I am to speak. But one night in New Zealand, I got caught empty-handed, wide awake in a bad dream. I was tired, the group contained every age imaginable, the topic was not the one they expected. And clearly, I was not connecting. Blank faces stared at me all around the room. I should add that New Zealanders are not southerners. When you finish, they don't make warm, fuzzy remarks to induce happy feelings. They are too genuine for that. This evening ended with long silences—buckets of polite silence.

> *Fear is truly the enemy of passion and a roadblock to the wisdom God would give us.*

I'm living through one of my worst nightmares, I remember thinking at the end. But you know, I survived. I survived one of my worst fears, and strangely enough, I've been less afraid of speaking in public ever since!

Fear is truly the enemy of passion and a roadblock to the wisdom God would give us. Fear often shows up in our lives in strange containers, I find. It's not unusual that a woman who seems fixated on managing her husband's or her children's lives is actually afraid to look at her own. Sometimes it's easier to worry over someone else's life than to grab hold of her own goals—to listen for God's call on *her* life. And so, what looks like too much advice is really just fear wearing a strange dress.

Fear can breed a kind of paralysis that makes you think you have to wait until the fear is gone to do the thing you need to do.

Even our prayers hint, sometimes, at the illusion of waiting to be unafraid. *Help me, Lord, to get past my fear so that I can love my husband better or apply for that job or talk with my father about his drunken tirades.* It's as though the actual doing must be put on hold until the fear evaporates. And so we wait . . . and we wait . . . and life passes us by.

When I spoke with Sue, it was clear she was tired of watching her life flow past her. If she was going to take the steps that would lead toward her dream of teaching, the time was now. But I could feel her fear of "taking a new step," as Dostoevsky would say, almost as though that fear could be bottled or touched by hand. The taboo against change or risk was just that strong. "What are you doing with the fear that can move you forward?" I asked her.

"Well, I am praying about it," she said. "I sense the gentle prodding of God, pulling me in this new direction. I'm scared—but I'm going." She began to make inquiries, got her teaching certification, and eventually, even interviewed with a few principals.

When I am tempted to let fear have the upper hand in my life, I think of Sue. It was clear to her that the gap between where she was and where she wanted to be was the place where God would meet her.

THE BIBLE AND FEAR

I can only conclude that fear is endemic to the human condition because the Bible speaks about fear so often. Every angelic appearance begins with the same three words: Do not fear. When Joshua was preparing to enter the Promised Land, God repeated to him over and over: Do not fear, for I am with you. I guess Joshua was having a few bad dreams too. Even in the New Testament, Paul's forceful personality did not cancel out his fear. He admitted to the Corinthians that all the time he was telling them about Jesus, he was there "in weakness and in fear and in much trembling."[1]

I find that comforting. Apparently, we are all standing outside the Garden of Eden, a bit like waifs in search of our true home. Perhaps when Hannah Hurnard wrote her famous allegory *Hinds' Feet on High Places,* she knew that naming her heroine Much Afraid would resonate with us all. Indeed, we are all afraid.

Not all the biblical references to fear imply it's something to be rid of, however. There is a good kind of fear. Wisdom actually begins with fearing God.[2] The idea is that we are meant to live in holy reverence of the living God—then, rather paradoxically, we have nothing to fear. Allowing the Lord to be our fear is what Dallas Willard calls "playing to an Audience of One."[3] God's eyes become the only ones that really matter. He becomes our safe place—a refuge from all the lesser things that would make our knees knock. As Isaiah says,

> It is the LORD of hosts whom you should regard as holy.
> And He shall be your fear,
> And He shall be your dread.
> Then He shall become a sanctuary.[4]

So there is such a thing as healthy fear. We should fear the King, and especially, we should fear evil. If you ever think about having an affair, for example, and you feel fear—listen to your fear. Part of wisdom is learning what to fear, and thereby, to keep your distance.

But most of us are like Sue, where the fear that stalks our souls and strangles the life of our hearts comes from resisting the gentle prodding of God to move out into life in some new way. We are afraid—not of evil, but of making fools of ourselves, of being less liked by others, of looking like a dolt. When we give in to this kind of fear and let it run our lives, we get stuck in a shrunken form of the life we are meant to have.

BEING TRAINED BY FEAR

There is an insidious nature to fear—it binds and restricts. Fear literally trains us. Sometimes, as in the case of sudden trauma, a visceral, automatic response known as PTSD, or posttraumatic stress disorder, is set in place. If you've ever had a car wreck, you remember how you recoiled at the thought of riding in another car. For the same reason, no one wants to touch a hot stove. Your brain remembers very well how badly that hurt.

The way our brains respond to pain is much like the way elephants are trained. A strong, short chain is roped around an elephant's neck and then attached to a post of some sort. The elephant learns that every time she pulls hard on the chain, her neck will ache. Being a good elephant, she doesn't forget. In short order, the post itself can be disconnected from the chain and removed entirely. Now, with only a chain around her neck, the elephant will stay in place for days—haunted by the memory of pain.

It's no wonder that in the larger picture of life, it takes courage and active trust to overcome real fear. Stepping out in a new way is no small thing. We have some memory of the last time our necks hurt, so to speak. When my daughter ached through a painful breakup with a man she thought she loved, I encouraged her to step back into the social scene fairly soon. See other men. Get back on the horse you were thrown from and ride. *To give place to fear is to accept its bondage.* In the words of Eleanor Roosevelt,

> You gain strength, courage, and confidence by every experience in which you really stop to look fear in the face. . . . You must do the thing you cannot do.

You must, by the grace of God, do the thing you cannot do. It becomes possible—in the actual doing of it. And what you gain from the blood and sweat and tears is a kind of wisdom you can't get any other way.

God follows the same pattern in our lives that he has hidden in the secret of the butterfly's cocoon. A cocoon is not the place of dark nothingness we think. A world of stuff is happening in there. In order to get out, this little creature must wrestle her way. The roll and tumble it takes for her to emerge—to bust her way out—is what builds sufficient strength in her wings to support the weight of flight. Without the struggle of the cocoon, the butterfly would be earthbound.

God knows that the strength that comes from wrestling with our fear will give us wings to fly.

Indeed, the movement of God in our lives is always to take us by the hand and walk us through the territory of our fear. Sometimes that feels like the adventure it is—other times, we are led there kicking and screaming. But God leads in that direction because it is the place of encounter with him.

It is worth noting that the most intimate conversation recorded in Scripture between God and an individual is occasioned by fear. When Job lost his family and his fortune, he said that the thing he always feared had come upon him. The Book of Job is the story of Job's wrestling—his frustration and his questioning, his stumbling attempts to make sense of it all. Eventually, God answers Job out of the storm. God tells him to stand up and talk like a man.

You must, by the grace of God, do the thing you cannot do.

Then, God lays out a stream of his own questions for Job. *Where were you, Job, when I enclosed the sea with doors and listened to the morning stars sing together for the sheer joy of it all?*[5] Job listens. He is brushed by the majesty and wonder of God. Job's immortal conclusion is that he had heard about God, but then he experienced him. There's a world of difference. And that encounter came through the door of his fears.

The case can be made that you don't really get to know God except by wading into your fear and discovering him there.

The same principle is seen in the New Testament. There is a race set before each of us, the author of Hebrews says. It's our own personal race and it matters how we run it. So we must jettison the things that weigh us down. Sin tangles up our feet and we need to let it go. But we must also "lay aside every encumbrance."[6] The particular set of fears and insecurities that bind our soul—these are encumbrances. As we move through life we are meant to let those go so that, more and more, we are free to run the race well. Contending with our fears shapes the story of our lives—literally, it gives us a story to tell.

> O Lord, surely I am Thy servant,
> I am Thy servant, . . .
> Thou hast loosed my bonds.

> Come and hear, all who fear God,
> And I will tell of what He has done for my soul.[7]

TACKLING YOUR FEAR

I keep a short quote by southern novelist Randall Kenan in my office, because in some histrionic way, it motivates me to confront my fear so as to unloose the passion and heart God has placed in me.

Kenan connects fear with shame. He says that much of our fear is about encountering something that might induce shame. And so he writes: "We are held—impaled, you might say—by what shames us and [that] becomes what compels us to the passionate life; we must transform it into creativity or flee from it forever in terror, leaving horrific destruction in our wake." What he means is that fear can literally unlock the creativity and passion in our hearts—if we are willing to walk into it with a bit of courage.

Walking into what you fear, though, has a few contingencies you want to plan for ahead of time.

You Will Hear Negative Voices in Your Head

To one degree or another, all of us have old tapes—a set of harsh voices in our mind. And the volume gets turned up in a big way when we walk in the direction of our fears. That is a given.

I know, for instance, that every time I face the blank, barren page of a new writing project, I will have to listen to the same old stuff. *How could you have something valid to say on this topic? Of all the audacity, Paula. Who do you think you are?* The old voices in my head are absurdly predictable. Sometimes I mosey along OK for a while, and I think I have overcome them permanently. But then, I will hit a new challenge that makes me feel particularly inadequate, and there they are again in the background—a barking, yelping pack of mongrels insisting that I give up and go home. I have to beat them off with a stick.

The good thing is that I know I'm not alone. Our insecurities are remarkably generic. A woman once explained to me how her fear had kept her from starting a program for kids with special needs—something she had longed to do for ages. But every time she began, the same old nagging stuff would start in her head. So she kept putting off the dream.

"So what do you hear in your mind?" I asked her.

"Don't do this—you'll just disappoint these kids. You really can't pull this off. You *have* gained ten pounds this year, you know" (as if that would disqualify anyone). And then the last and most classic: "What is wrong with you?" That was the litany that my friend encountered whenever she got close to actually doing the thing she felt led to do—but was scared to do.

Does this sound at all familiar? What are the crazy old tapes that begin to play in your head when fear pushes the "on" button? It's really one of the great tasks of your life to learn how to talk back, and to discover that these negative tapes are not the voice of God. As Nicole Johnson says,

> These voices keep our souls chained in the basement. They make us fearful to try anything new, anxious about what others may think of us, and they keep us on the treadmill of performance. In short, if we allow them, these voices can easily rob every ounce of enjoyment from the lives we have. Many women don't even know they are giving power to the voices, living in a state of constant self-disapproval. Understand this: these voices can immobilize us and keep us from dreaming our dreams. They can discourage us and cause us to think too small and expect too little from our lives. . . . They make us afraid to be who we are. The voices can keep us from writing books or changing careers or loving our children well.
>
> But only if we let them.[8]

Without a doubt, being able to banish these negative tapes hinges on realizing in a deep way that these voices are not the voice of God. He simply does not talk like that to his children. God speaks with infinite tenderness. He corrects with relentless compassion. Listen to his words, spoken through the prophet Isaiah:

> Do not fear, for I am with you;
> Do not anxiously look about you, for I am your God.
> I will strengthen you, surely I will help you,
> Surely I will uphold you with My righteous right hand.[9]

It must cause God no small grief that we so easily project our fear and self-condemnation onto him—as though that is the way *he* feels about us. "You thought that I was altogether like you," he challenges.[10] So the chronic disapproval and the harshness we feel toward ourselves become the feelings we assume God shares. Those projections blind us to the real awareness of his comforting, enabling presence in the midst of the muddle that is our lives. He is there—but we can't sense him.

I often think of the half-humorous way that author and spiritual director Brennan Manning says he talks to his neuroses in the morning when he first gets up. "I dialogue with my neuroses and ask whether they are acutely agitated today, in which case I offer them my empathy—or just in their normal debilitating state, in which case I rely on my regular supply of compassion."[11]

Isn't that wonderful? What Brennan is saying is that we must divorce the cranky, demanding voices in our heads from the voice of God—and we do that by offering our own souls a measure of empathy and compassion. It is the empathy and compassion that Jesus, himself, would offer us.

It is good to remember that God's word to us comes in straight-forward declarations about who we are and how he sees us in Christ. You are a child of God, redeemed by the blood of Christ, lavished by his grace. You are. You are. You just are—because God declares you are. There is nothing to do but lay claim to who you are in Christ.

But the enemy of our souls comes to us in a different manner, amazingly similar to the way he came to Jesus in the wilderness. Do you remember how he talked to Christ? "If You are the Son of God, command that these stones become bread."[12] *If you are . . .* that is the key phrase. The enemy challenges us at the bedrock level of our identities. Who we are is not something to rest in and thank God for. It is something to be proved—over and over and over. *If you are . . .* this is one way in which we distinguish the negative tapes in our heads from the actual voice of God.

It Will Always Feel Like Risk

As much as we might wish otherwise, fear and doubt remain in the picture of our lives. Even for mature and talented and godly people, faith includes fear. There is always an element of risk.

The bogeyman of fear does not shrink by some kind of magic wand that vaporizes the feeling. We don't see the waters of the Nile part in any real way until we actually stick our feet in the water. Abraham left Ur not knowing where he was going—surely he felt a bit afraid. Peter wanted Jesus to assure him that his life would be like John's and he had nothing to fear. Jesus said simply, "Follow me."

I am often drawn to Mary's life as she faced the prospect of bearing a child out of wedlock, whose origins no one could fathom at that point. All the elements that most elicit my fear were her experience: Facing the unexpected, the total unknown,

Obedience goes before our hearts and carries them where they would not normally go.

being misunderstood by everyone around her. God asked her, simply and inexorably, to trust him. I find that pattern to be true: Obedience goes before our hearts and carries them where they would not normally go.

What I'm really saying is that God doesn't erase fear from the blackboard of our lives. Rather, he grows our souls by the sometimes hugely uncomfortable experience of trusting him as we do the thing that's frightening. And we discover him there, in it all. As Joyce Meyer explains, we don't wait until we have overcome fear to move out as God wants us to. Her word of encouragement is, "Do it afraid."[13]

Corrie Ten Boom, a Dutch Holocaust survivor, wrote about the Nazi concentration camps where her family was sent for harboring Jews in World War II. During the early years of the war, Corrie lived with the fear that her family would eventually be discovered by the Nazis. She sought her father's advice. What would she do if the Nazis came to search their home? How would she handle it?

Her father recalled for her the memory of being at a busy railway station, as a little girl, waiting for the train to come. "When did I give you the ticket to board the train?" he asked. "Didn't I give you the ticket you needed right before you got on board?" Corrie understood. God would give her the grace she needed—the ticket—when the time came.[14]

That's such an accurate picture of what God does for each of us as we step in the direction of our fears. He enables us in the midst of moving forward. He gives us the ticket as we begin to board the train.

As long as we remain alive on the planet, faith will include fear. That we are afraid is not a mark of being insufficient to the task or made of inferior stuff. Risk is always part of the package. As Gerald May explains,

> Because real risking in faith can occur only in those areas of life where we feel most impoverished and vulnerable, it never becomes something we are really comfortable with. For each layer of trust that builds up, another, more challenging risk is offered. True faith choices, therefore, always feel like risks; they just go on, involving deeper and deeper levels of our being. Each choice remains difficult; what really becomes conditioned in this process is simply our willingness and readiness to take the risks of faith. They never stop feeling like risks.[15]

Dostoevsky said that taking a new step or uttering a new word—as simple as that sounds—is, indeed, what we fear most. When you are tackling something that feels new and uncharted, it helps to do two things: Take small steps and then, let yourself celebrate their significance. Doing anything new is like knitting a sweater, one row at a time. It builds on itself. After a while you have strung together one new step with another new step until you are in a different place. To celebrate the significance of that as you go along helps you continue to trust God.

The small steps that Sue took have pieced together the dream she always carried inside her. She is teaching middle-school students—and loving it. It feels like something she was always meant to do. But she admits that she is on the biggest learning curve of her life. "I hate being forty and feeling so inadequate every day," she says. Her mother recently came to visit. And while she admires her daughter's spunk, she sees how hard the first year of teaching is and she says, "I bet you're sorry. I bet you wish you'd never left your old position." From the restricted world of the deaf, her mom projects her own fear onto her daughter.

"Honestly, Mom, I'm not sorry I did this," her daughter replies. "This year is hard—but I know this is where I'm supposed to be."

It helps to celebrate the hurdles you have crossed to get where you are—in order to face well the ones that are now in front of you. Wisdom is found along a path that is strewn with our own sets of fears and insecurities to be faced. We must do the thing we think we cannot do.

It's in the doing that the strength comes.

Listen with Your Heart

1. Everyone has a set of fears and insecurities that hold them hostage. How would you rank these potential fears?

   - Confronting a friend or coworker

   - NOT overhelping, caretaking, fixing a spouse or close friend

   - Losing your job

   - Speaking in public

   - Risking your child's anger with you

   - Entering a new social experience alone

   - Seeming inadequate before a friend or coworker

   - Other_____

2. Of your two top-ranked fears, which causes you the most concern? Which holds you back the most? Why?

3. In what ways are your fears and insecurities the enemy of passion, the thing that strangles the life of your heart?

4. How does fear affect your spiritual life?

5. If your fear assumed a voice (which it does), what would it say to you? What does the harsh negative message in your mind sound like?

6. What would Christ say to you? What would his words of comfort and encouragement sound like?

7. Read Deuteronomy 31:6. What is God saying here about himself that can change the face of your fear?

8. Read Isaiah 41:10. What is God promising to do?

9. Sarah, the wife of Abraham, is remembered for her courage in the face of her husband's misjudgments and her willingness to leave the land of her birth, setting out in faith for a land God had promised to give. What do you learn from her about the relationship between fear and trust in 1 Peter 3:3–6?

10. If you took the step of faith God is prompting in you, what would it look like to "do it afraid"?

12

LONGING FOR RESOLUTION

For all that has been, thank you; for all that will be, yes.

DAG HAMMARSKJÖLD

So teach us to number our days,
That we may present to Thee a heart of wisdom.

PSALM 90:12

So we return to the central question before us, and that is: How do we make this journey with the Lord without leaving our hearts behind somewhere on the trail?

I would suggest to you that making the journey well, with your heart intact, hinges on how you see the big picture of your life. How does the story end? Do the broken pieces ever really come back together? Is there resolution of some sort? For if there is, then it may actually be both safe and wise to bring your heart along for the ride.

As I listen to women talk about their lives, their heart cry is often about this longing for resolution. Not so much for a happy ending, really, but for some deep assurance that someone who loves them is painting on a large canvas and even the darker, stormier colors are somehow needed. If they knew that in their bones, somehow they could rest. The child who is lost on drugs or the husband who died unexpectedly in surgery or their lifelong struggle with depression would not be "all she wrote." The end of the story. And that would make all the difference in the world.

One of the lines from a novel by Edith Wharton expresses the way many of us secretly see our stories and the utter humanness of it all. She writes,

> What I meant was that when you've lived a little longer you'll see what complex blunderers we all are: how we're struck blind sometimes, and mad sometimes—and then, when our sight and our senses come back, how we have to set to work, and build up, little by little, bit by bit, the precious things we'd smashed to atoms without knowing it. *Life's just a perpetual piecing together of broken bits.* (emphasis mine)

Isn't that at least part of the simple truth? We are "complex blunderers" and we live with complex blunderers—and before we have journeyed far, there is a pile of precious things in pieces at our feet. And sometimes, the heart is one of those precious things. We try—mightily—to glue the shreds of it all back together, but really, our longing goes so much deeper. A peculiar hope tugs at our coattails, taps us on the shoulder, dogs our steps. A hope that what we have been told is actually true: Some greater transformation—a true healing—will take place. And quite apart from our own efforts.

We long to believe that God is writing a bigger story from our lives than we could possibly imagine—that all our past is indeed "Thank you," and all our future is "Yes."

I will tell you how, on some heart level, the reality of this resolution came through to me personally. But to do that well, I have to give you a bit of my father's story.

The huge broken piece of his life took place on a warm October day in 1936 when his mother and his sister and her child were killed in a car wreck. My father was the driver. The naïve and tender innocence of his twenty-one years vanished nearly overnight—and he lived the rest of his adult life with the guilty shadow of those untimely deaths.

Had you known him in his prime, you would never have guessed, though. He had a thoroughly contagious sense of humor, a bedrock faith. That Christ was truth incarnate was, as he liked to put it, "the ultimate truth of the universe." He spent fifty years as a small-town banker—same town, same bank. You could find him there most any day talking with merchants and farmers he'd known forever. I used to stop by the bank after school so I could catch him up on my day—not realizing that from behind this cloud of smoke (he was never without a cigarette) he was dispensing a kind of warmth and home-grown wisdom that would form my best memories.

A peculiar hope tugs at our coattails, taps us on the shoulder, dogs our steps. A hope that what we have been told is actually true.

Now fast-forward to the last ten years of my father's life. The nightmare of the earlier tragedy returned in dreams and conscious thought in a way that my father could not shake. His personality took on strange peculiarities. He was not his old self, and the man he became we hardly recognized. Visit after visit, he got a little worse, declining by slow degrees over a long period of time. The best that can be said for this part of our family history is that we endured. We barely remembered the man he once was. Congestive heart failure, the doctors said, would end this saga.

The last few months of my father's life, I had taken to calling him every night or so. Always, it was a brief, nearly nonsensical conversation, but I called. One night, though, when I was particularly rushed, I phoned him—and this time, he dropped the phone. I called back and he spoke into the wrong end of the receiver. I had almost decided to give up and try another day, except that I felt a gentle prodding. *Try him one more time, Paula.*

This time the strangest thing happened. The man who spoke to me on the other line was as close as you can imagine to the father I once knew. Even the tone of his voice was the same. He called me by my childhood name. "Paula Sue, I love you," he said. "I always knew when you grew up you would be a wonderful girl." And that was it.

He died three days later. But what had transpired between us was the heart equivalent of being handed a small bouquet of roses by someone right before they slip behind a curtain. It was not so much a reminder of the past as it was a tiny peek into the future. There was the slightest hint of the first shreds of restoration, of healing, of life about to begin.

I could sense how surely all that we've enjoyed and lost—or longed for and never quite realized—will be ours in spades. John Updike once remarked that he knew others saw the universe as a freak show, and while he had never had some big vision of God, he had, as he said, "heard whispers from the wings of the stage." That's what I heard in those moments—whispers from the wings of the stage. And it sounded very, very good.

SAYING "YES" TO LIFE

What does this have to do with my heart, you say? A little bit of everything, really. For the more certain it is to you that God is painting on a big canvas and the picture is going to be beautiful beyond the telling—the more willing you will be to hang in for the long haul. The greater strength with which you'll walk out your days. The more possible it will be for you to offer to the Lord, as Moses said, a heart of wisdom.

I am writing, of course, about heaven. But I am hesitant to say the word for fear you will get lost in harps and halos and miss the real point: You can live in the present moment with your heart open and alive—saying "Yes" to life—because your future looks really bright. In Christ, your way home has been prepared. It's interesting that when C. S. Lewis tried to communicate our longing for resolution—for heaven—he turned to the metaphor of story. At the end of his series of children's fiction, all his characters die in a railway accident and Lewis concludes with these words:

> But the things that began to happen after that were so great and so beautiful that I cannot write them. And for us this is the end of all the stories . . . but for them it was only the beginning of the real story. All their life in this world and all their adventures in Narnia had only been the cover and the title page: now at last they were beginning Chapter One of the Great Story, which no one on earth has read, which goes on forever, in which every chapter is better than the one that came before.[1]

What difference would it make in your life if all your losses—all the disappointment and aggravation life can throw your way—were, in your mind, only the cover and the title page to your real story? Wouldn't trusting God be something your heart would absolutely run toward?

I wonder, sometimes, if we don't carry an invisible pendulum in our souls. And the more clearly we see the horizon out there—where resolution, transformation, healing will truly happen—the less we need for our plans and agendas to work out now. The light moves on the stage of our lives, and what presently looks so incomplete and half-baked pales beside what is to come. Heaven does not seem like a consolation prize to noble losers in this life, but rather, some great secret the Lord has let us in on. If, as God told Job, when the world was created all the morning stars sang together and the angels shouted for joy, then what in heaven's name will the marriage feast of the Lamb be like? How will it feel to shine like lights in the kingdom of our Father?

All this talk of resolution, of heaven, would seem to minimize your life in the present tense. But strangely enough, it works the other way. The future riddles the here and now with meaning. It frees your heart to actually live.

There is a particular image I want to leave with you that symbolizes the freedom and passion of heart I think God invites us to in this life. The story comes out of the last century, from the life of John Muir, a famous explorer of the Pacific Northwest. For decades, Muir tramped up and down the rugged territory from the California Sierras to the Alaskan glaciers, entering into whatever he found there with a kind of childlike delight and appreciation. He thrived on experiencing this great yet-uncharted land.

If God has you in the palm of his hand and your real life is secure in him, then you can venture forth . . . and you will be safe there.

One December day a storm blew in from the Pacific—the kind that bent the junipers and pines like so many blades of grass. Everyone retreated to their cabins to sit beside cozy fires, wrapped in sheepskins. But Muir pulled the door tight behind him and strode out of the cabin, into the storm. He climbed a high ridge and chose a giant Douglas fir for a perch from where he experienced the whole show—all the color and sound, scent and motion he could take in, holding on for dear life.[2]

If God has you in the palm of his hand and your real life is secure in him, then you can venture forth—into the places and relationships, the challenges, the very heart of the storm—and you will be safe there. I have no idea where God will lead as the cabin door shuts behind you. Perhaps you will find yourself like our friends who sold the family business and moved to Calcutta to help some folks discover Christ and start cottage industries. Or maybe your perch will be more like mine, right on my own street, entering into the life God has for me here—for all I'm worth. I only know that life with him is about this venturing forth and taking your heart along for the trip.

There are only three options for approaching life, Gerald May wrote in his book *Addiction and Grace*. We can deny the call of God on our lives or just pretend the call isn't there. Or we can try to claim control of the shape and form our lives will take. The third option, he says, is the courageous attempt "to face life in a truly undefended and open-ended way." He is speaking of this willingness to take our perch in the Douglas fir—where the real stuff is happening and we know we aren't the ones in control. Where trusting God is indeed the only agenda that makes any sense at all. It is a posture of "gracious uncertainty,"[3] meaning that we have given up the illusion of being certain of anything but God.

In this place of gracious uncertainty, we wait. For the broken pieces to be brought back together. For the meaning of our suffering to be revealed in his. For the righteous reign of a mighty God, whose goodness we will spend all eternity celebrating. We wait—with open, expectant hearts.

Waiting does not diminish us, any more than waiting diminishes a pregnant mother. We are enlarged in the waiting. We, of course, don't see what is enlarging us. But the longer we wait . . . the more joyful our expectancy.[4]

Listen with Your Heart

1. When do you most feel the ache of longing for resolution, for the broken pieces of life to be knit back together?

2. Read in Romans 8:18–39 Paul's effusive words on the glory that will one day be revealed. Note as many things as you can find that are being anticipated in all the groaning and waiting that is spoken of in this passage.

3. Write about the part that encourages you the most.

4. In what ways does this encourage you to say "Yes" to life now?

5. What difference would it make in your life if all your losses, disappointments, and aggravations were something you saw as the cover and the title page of your real story?

6. What would it mean in your life to claim your perch in the Douglas fir? What would that look like?

Notes

Chapter 1

1. Jeremiah 17:9.
2. Herb Gardner, *A Thousand Clowns* (New York: Random House, 1962).
3. See Luke 12:15 and John 4:13–14.
4. My thanks to Sally Breedlove for first describing a woman's life to me in this particularly appropriate metaphor.
5. See Psalm 27:4.
6. From a poem by George Herbert (1593–1633), title unknown.
7. Philip Yancey, *Reaching for the Invisible God* (Grand Rapids, Mich.: Zondervan, 2000), 201.
8. Brennan Manning, *Ruthless Trust* (San Francisco: HarperSanFrancisco, 2000), 2.
9. Brent Curtis and John Eldredge, *Sacred Romance* (Nashville: Thomas Nelson, 1997), 45.
10. Isaiah 55:2, 3.

Chapter 2

1. Nicole Johnson, *Fresh-Brewed Life* (Nashville: Thomas Nelson, 1999), 45.

2. Zechariah 12:1.

3. John Eldredge, *The Journey of Desire* (Nashville: Thomas Nelson, 2000), 36.

4. See Matthew 20:29–34.

5. Eldredge, *The Journey of Desire*, 36.

6. C. S. Lewis, *The Screwtape Letters* (New York: Macmillan, 1961), 59.

7. Proverbs 14:12 (NKJV), emphasis added.

8. Eldredge, *The Journey of Desire*, 59.

9. Gerald G. May, *Addiction and Grace* (San Francisco: Harper & Row, 1988), 30.

10. Nicole Johnson explores further the pitfalls of being a "spectator" in her book *Fresh-Brewed Life.*

11. Psalm 37:4.

12. May, *Addiction and Grace*, 179–180.

Chapter 3

1. A. E. Housman, "When I Was One and Twenty" (public domain)

2. Janet Fitch, *White Oleander* (Boston: Little, Brown, 1999).

Chapter 4

1. See Habakkuk 3:19.

2. Hannah Hurnard, *Hinds' Feet on High Places* (London: The Olive Press, 1955).

3. See Proverbs 4:23.

4. Frederick Buechner, *Telling Secrets* (San Francisco: HarperSanFrancisco, 1991), 3, 45.

5. Genesis 3:10.

6. Anne Lamott, *Bird by Bird: Some Instructions on Writing and Life* (New York: Doubleday, 1994), 29.

7. Dan B. Allender, *The Healing Path* (Colorado Springs: WaterBrook Press, 1999), 26.

8. John 1:16.

9. Jeremiah 17:5–6.

10. Psalm 27:13.

11. George MacDonald, *Phantastes* (New York: Schocken Books, 1982).

12. John Eldredge explains this sequence in his Sacred Romance seminar.

13. Saint John of the Cross, arranged and paraphrased by David Hazard, *You Set My Spirit Free* (Minneapolis, Minn.: Bethany House, 1994).

14. Saint John of the Cross, *You Set My Spirit Free.*

Chapter 5

1. Eldredge, *The Journey of Desire*, 97.

2. C. S. Lewis, *A Grief Observed* (Toronto: Bantam, 1961), 61.

3. 1 Corinthians 2:9 (NKJV).

4. C. S. Lewis, *The Problem of Pain* (New York: Macmillan, 1962), 115.

5. Hosea 2:14–16.

6. As quoted by Richard Foster, *Prayer: Finding the Heart's True Home* (San Francisco: HarperSanFrancisco, 1992), 54.

Chapter 6

1. See Ephesians 3:17–19.

2. See Luke 15:11–32.

3. Malachi 4:2.

4. M. Craig Barnes, *Yearning* (Downers Grove, Ill.: InterVarsity Press, 1992), 106.

5. As told by Brennan Manning, *Ruthless Trust*, 5.

6. Dale Hanson Bourke, *Turn Toward the Wind* (Grand Rapids, Mich.: Zondervan Publishing House, 1995).

7. Manning, *Ruthless Trust*, 60.

8. Curtis and Eldredge, *Sacred Romance*, 155.

9. Psalm 23:6 (KJV).

10. John Piper, *The Pleasure of God* (Portland, Oreg.: Multnomah, 1991), 189, 191.

Chapter 7

1. Proverbs 31:10.

2. Cynthia and Robert Hicks, *The Feminine Journey* (Colorado Springs: Navpress, 1994), 167.

3. William C. Placher, *Narratives of a Vulnerable God* (Louisville, Ky.: Westminster / John Knox Press, 1994), 8.

4. From a retreat seminar by Brennan Manning.

5. Deuteronomy 4:9.

6. Johnson, *Fresh-Brewed Life*, 30.

7. Psalm 51:6.

8. C. S. Lewis, *The Letters of C. S. Lewis to Arthur Greeves* (New York: Collier Books, 1979), 104.

9. Henri J. M. Nouwen, *The Way of the Heart* (New York: Ballantine, 1981), 15.

10. T. S. Eliot, "The Love Song of J. Alfred Prufrock," *The Complete Poems and Plays, 1909–1950* (New York: Harcourt, Brace & Co., 1952), 8.

11. Frederick Buechner, *A Room Called Remember* (New York: Harper & Row, 1984), 48.

12. 1 John 1:7.

13. Barnes, *Yearning,* 89, 93.

14. Matthew 11:28–30.

Chapter 8

1. See the parable of Christ in Matthew 18:21–35.

2. Harriet Goldhor Lerner, *The Dance of Anger* (New York: Harper & Row, 1985)196.

3. See Matthew 5:23–24.

4. Hebrews 12:15.

5. Isaiah 61:7–8; 49:4 (AV).

6. Joel 2:25 (NKJV).

7. Romans 12:19.

8. Sandra Wilson, *Into Abba's Arms* (Wheaton, Ill: Tyndale House, 1998).

9. From Novie Hinson's seminar on forgiveness, as told in Brenda Hunter's book *In the Company of Women* (Sisters, Oreg.: Multnomah, 1994).

10. Lewis Smedes, *Forgive and Forget* (San Francisco: Harper & Row, 1984), 47.

11. Romans 12:18.

12. "An Interview with Anne Lamott," *Clarity Magazine,* February/March 2000.

13. Proverbs 28:13 (NIV).

14. My thanks to Bill Thrall and his colleagues at Leadership Catalyst for their helpful insight into the distinction between being sinless and being blameless before God.

Chapter 9

1. Wendy Shalit, *A Return to Modesty* (New York: Free Press, 1999).

2. Linda Dillow and Lorraine Pintus, *Intimate Issues* (Colorado Springs: WaterBrook Press, 1999), 14.

3. 1 Corinthians 7:4–5.

4. Alain Boublil, Herbert Kretzmer, Mourou Lucchetti, Claude-Michel Schoenberg, "I Dreamed a Dream" (NY: Alain Boublil Music Ltd., 1985).

5. Genesis 24:67.

6. George Gilder, *Men and Marriage* (Gretna, La.: Pelican Publishing Co., 1986) 10–11.

7. See Colossians 1:27.

8. See Ephesians 3:8–9.

9. Ephesians 5:31–32.

10. John Donne, *Holy Sonnet 14* (public domain).

11. 1 Corinthians 6:12–20.

Chapter 10

1. Colossians 1:13 (MSG).

2. Romans 5:3–5.

3. John 13:35.

4. Ecclesiastes 4:9–10, 12.

5. Mike Mason, *The Mystery of Marriage* (Portland, Oreg.: Multnomah, 1978), 141–142.

6. Psalm 119:32 (KJV).

7. 1 John 2:9.

8. Henri J. M. Nouwen, *Lifesigns* (New York: Seabury, 1981).

Chapter 11

1. 1 Corinthians 2:3.
2. Proverbs 1:7.
3. Dallas Willard, *The Divine Conspiracy* (San Francisco: HarperSanFrancisco, 1998).
4. Isaiah 8:13–14.
5. See Job 38—42.
6. Hebrews 12:1.
7. Psalm 116:16; 66:16.
8. Johnson, *Fresh-Brewed Life*, 38.
9. Isaiah 41:10.
10. Psalm 50:21 (NKJV).
11. From a retreat led by Brennan Manning.
12. Matthew 4:3.
13. Joyce Meyer, *Beauty for Ashes* (Tulsa, Okla.: Harrison House, 1994).
14. Corrie ten Boom, *The Hiding Place* (Washington Depot, Conn.: Chosen Books, 1971).
15. May, *Addiction and Grace*, 130.

Chapter 12

1. C. S. Lewis, *The Last Battle* (New York: MacMillan Publishing, 1952).
2. Eugene Petersen tells Muir's story particularly well in the Foreword to *Water My Soul,* by Luci Shaw (Grand Rapids: Zondervan, 1998).
3. Oswald Chambers, *My Utmost for His Highest* (New York: Dodd, Mead & Co., 1935), April 29.
4. Romans 8:24–25 (MSG).

About the Author

P aula Rinehart has touched women's lives through writing, speaking, and personal ministry for more than twenty years. The author of four books, Paula speaks at women's conferences and leads retreats focused on personal growth and intimacy with Christ. She lives with her husband, Stacy, in Raleigh, North Carolina, where she also works as a professional counselor.

To contact Paula, you may write her at 8720 Hidden View Court, Raleigh, NC 27613 or e-mail her at stacyrinehart@compuserve.com.